The Multinational Businessman and Foreign Policy

Jeffrey M. Brookstone

The Praeger Special Studies program—utilizing the most modern and efficient book production techniques and a selective worldwide distribution network—makes available to the academic, government, and business communities significant, timely research in U.S. and international economic, social, and political development.

The Multinational Businessman and Foreign Policy

Entrepreneurial Politics in East-West Trade and Investment

PRAEGER SPECIAL STUDIES IN INTERNATIONAL BUSINESS, FINANCE, AND TRADE

Praeger Publishers   New York   Washington   London

382.3
B 823

Library of Congress Cataloging in Publication Data

Brookstone, Jeffrey M
    The multinational businessman and foreign policy.

    (Praeger special studies in international business,
finance, and trade)
    Bibliography: p. 158
    Includes index.
    1. United States—Commercial policy.   2. Businessmen—
United States—Political activity.   3. International business
enterprises.   4. Corporations, American.   I. Title.
HF1455.B73   382'.3'0973   76-12845
ISBN 0-275-23360-X

PRAEGER PUBLISHERS
111 Fourth Avenue, New York, N.Y. 10003, U.S.A.

Published in the United States of America in 1976
by Praeger Publishers, Inc.

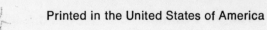

Printed in the United States of America

For

Paul H. Douglas
Distinguished Economic Scholar
and
Humble Public Servant

FOREWORD
Phillip D. Grub

The Multinational Businessman and Foreign Policy is a case
study of East-West trade and investment. Written during a time
of critical reassessment of U. S. -USSR detente politics, this book
illustrates constraints of U. S. foreign policy when applied to the
overseas corporate strategies of U. S. multinational business
operations.

The author presents two very significant messages. First,
American business should play a formal and direct role in key U.S.
foreign policy issue-areas of East-West trade and investment.
Second, the development of a field of study in entrepreneurial politics
is long overdue. Writers and scholars in international business and
politics can utilize role theory to explain the contribution U.S.
multinationals can make toward the conduct of U.S. foreign policy.

The role played by multinational corporate officers in the conduct
and implementation of U.S. foreign policy is significant and timely.
Never before in the history of U.S. business has the need for government-business cooperation been so pronounced. For example, in
the Soviet bloc nations of Eastern Europe, Japanese and West German
companies are outcompeting U.S. firms for product and technology
sales in many fields. To meet this challenge, U.S. diplomats and
businessmen need to complement each other's expertise. Consequently, U.S. businessmen must become knowledgeable political
actors. The critical appraisal of the East-West trade and investment issues contained in this book should help to facilitate this
development.

This book describes a variety of roles U.S. multinational
businessmen accept in confronting contemporary issues of East-West
foreign policy. In reviewing these issues, U.S. business and government executives will find this volume helpful for planning purposes,
while it serves as a most useful research resource for scholars in
the fields of business, political science, and international affairs.

ACKNOWLEDGMENTS

This study received generous support from The George Washington University and from the Woodrow Wilson International Center for Scholars, The Smithsonian Institution, Washington, D.C., where the writer served as a research associate from September 1974 until July 1975. The support was in the form of a graduate fellowship. Several distinguished international scholars contributed to shaping my interests in this research. They included Dr. Egon Sohmen and Dr. George F. Kennan. Professor Raymond Hopkins and Dr. Zed David provided helpful encouragement and support through the initial phases of the research.

I am especially indebted to Professor Phillip D. Grub, president of the Academy of International Business, for the patience and feedback in elaboration of the research and evaluation of the finished product. His concern over the contribution U.S. multinational executives make to the United States' political well-being is an example of invaluable civic responsibility.

A special thanks to James Mosel, professor of psychology at the George Washington University. He brought to my attention the methodological limitations of social science research.

Dr. Burton Sapin, dean of the School of Public and International Affairs, The George Washington University, was kind enough to provide me with insight into the complexities of U.S. foreign policy decision making. His expertise was deeply appreciated.

To the U.S. corporate executives and government officials who agreed to participate in this research by spending valuable hours in interviews, I am most grateful.

My greatest debt is to my wife, Lynne, who shared the joys and adversities involved with completing this research.

CONTENTS

Page

FOREWORD
Phillip D. Grub   vi

ACKNOWLEDGMENTS   vii

LIST OF TABLES   xi

LIST OF FIGURES   xiii

LIST OF ABBREVIATIONS   xiv

Chapter

1   THE ROLE OF U. S. MULTINATIONAL BUSINESSMEN
    IN THE CONDUCT OF U. S. FOREIGN POLICY   1

        Assumptions   3
        Scope of the Study   5
        Definitions   7
        Role Types   14
        Notes   18

2   THE RESEARCH FRAMEWORK   20

        The Meaning of Roles   21
        The Nature of Role Behavior   22
        The Role Actions of U. S. MNBs in the Conduct
          of Foreign Policy   24
        A Research Model   27
        Notes   39

3   U. S. MNBs' INPUT INTO EAST-WEST TRADE
    AND INVESTMENT POLICIES   40

        An Overview of Contemporary U. S. Policy   40
        Policy Making in Foreign Affairs   42
        Detente: The Problems and Prospects   43

Chapter		Page

U. S. MNBs' Input into East-West Trade and
Investment Policies   48
Notes   59

4   U. S. MULTINATIONAL BUSINESSMEN AS
POLITICAL ACTORS   61

U. S. Multinational Enterprises in the International
Political System   61
The Nature of Contemporary U. S. Diplomacy   63
The U. S. MNB as Political Actor   68
Attributes of U. S. Diplomats   75
Attributes of U. S. MNBs   77
The Professional Generalist Manager   82
U. S. MNBs' Role in East-West Politics   84
Notes   85

5   EAST-WEST TRADE AND INVESTMENT ISSUES   88

Commodity Trading with the Soviet Union and the
Eastern Bloc Countries   88
Export Licensing Problems on Eastern European
Sales   101
The Fairchild-Unitra Case   106
Future U. S. Investment in the Soviet-Bloc
Economies   110
Notes   117

6   MULTINATIONAL EXECUTIVE ROLES AND
EAST-WEST POLICIES   120

Executive-Bureaucratic Interactions on East-West
Trade and Investment Issues   121
Direct, Formal Participation of U. S. MNBs in
East-West Trade and Investment Issues   122
Direct, Informal Participation of U. S. MNBs in
East-West Trade and Investment Issues   132
Informal, Direct Participation of U. S. MNBs in
East-West Trade and Investment Issues   138
Informal, Indirect Participation of U. S. MNBs in
East-West Trade and Investment Issues   141
The Roles MNBs Play in the Conduct of U. S.
Foreign Policy   142
Notes   145

Chapter   Page

7   SUMMARY AND CONCLUSIONS   146

       Implications of the Study: Policy Aspects   148
       Implications of Entrepreneurial Politics
          as a Field of Study   150

APPENDIXES

A   Dr. C. Lester Hogan's Recommended Reforms of
          the Export License Control Process   153
B   Types of Cooperation Arrangements, by Robert
          Starr   155

BIBLIOGRAPHY   158

INDEX   173

ABOUT THE AUTHOR   185

LIST OF TABLES

Table   Page

1.1   Channels of Corporate Influence   5

2.1   MNCs Ranked by 1974 Sales   28

2.2   MNBs' Perspective—MNBs' Roles in the Conduct
      of U.S. Foreign Policy   30

2.3   Bureaucratic Perspective—MNBs' Roles in the Conduct
      of U.S. Foreign Policy   31

2.4   MNB Interview Sample   32

2.5   MNBs by Age Group   33

2.6   MNBs and Present Job Experience   33

2.7   MNBs and Education   34

2.8   MNBs and Job Responsibilities   34

2.9   U.S. Government Personnel in East-West Trade Field   35

2.10 Bureaucrats by Age Group   36

2.11 Bureaucrats and Present Job Experience   36

2.12 Bureaucrats by GS Rating   37

2.13 Bureaucrats and Education   37

2.14 Bureaucrats and Job Responsibilities   37

3.1   1973 Trade Results with Western Industrialized
      Nations   45

3.2   U.S.-USSR Trade, by Major Commodity Groups,
      1966-73   50

3.3   U.S. Exports and Imports from Communist Countries,
      1967 to September 1974   51

3.4   U.S. Direct Investments Abroad, by Area and
      Major Industry, 1960-71   52

5.1   Exports of U.S. Agricultural Commodities to
      Eastern Europe, by Commodity, 1967/68 - 1973/74   92

5.2   Exports of U.S. Agricultural Commodities to
      Eastern Europe, by Country, 1967/68 - 1973/74   93

5.3   USSR: Grain and Wheat Balances, 1970/71, and
      Projections for 1975/76, 1980/81, 1985/86   95

xi

Table		Page
5.4	USSR: Balance of Food Requirements and Domestic Supplies in Oat-Equivalent Feed Units, 1970/71, and Projections for 1975/76, 1980/81, and 1985/86	96
5.5	The Eastern European Semiconductor Market, 1973-80	106
5.6	Demand for Materials, 1951-2000, U.S., Japan, USSR, China	112
5.7	USSR Loans—Eximbank Direct and Unguaranteed Private Sources, March 1973-March 1974	112
5.8	Distribution of East-West Industrial Cooperation by Industrial Branches	115
6.1	Nature of MNBs' Contacts	123
6.2	Nature of U.S. Government Officials' Contacts with U.S. MNBs	124
6.3	Bureaucrats' Contact with U.S. MNCs	125
6.4	MNBs' Contacts with Competitor MNCs	126
6.5	Source of Policy Differences	127
6.6	Methods Used to Resolve Policy Differences	127
6.7	Activities Engaged in by Respondents in Changing East-West Trade Policy	128
6.8	Types of MNBs Contacting Government Officials	129
6.9	Former Government Officials Employed by MNCs	129
6.10	Contribution of Former Bureaucrats According to Multinational Businessmen	130
6.11	Contribution of MNBs Evaluated by Bureaucrats	131
6.12	MNBs' Intermediaries Utilized by Indirect, Formal Participation in Foreign Policy	132
6.13	Groups Used by U.S. MNBs to Effect Changes in U.S. Government Export Licensing Policy	133
6.14	MNBs Influencing Export Licenses	135
6.15	MNBs Influencing East-West Investment Policies	136
6.16	Groups Used by U.S. MNBs to Effect Changes in U.S. Government Investment Policy in Eastern Europe	137

Table		Page
6.17	MNBs' Informal, Direct Ties with Bureaucrats	138
6.18	Factors Promoting Similarity of Background Between Bureaucrats and U.S. MNBs	139
6.19	MNBs' Participation in East-West Trade Policies— Informal, Direct Ties	140
6.20	Roles MNBs Feel They Play in U.S. Foreign Policy	142
6.21	Roles Bureaucrats Feel MNBs Play in U.S. Foreign Policy	143

LIST OF FIGURES

Figure   Page

1   Structure of East-West Policy Making in U. S.
       Government   49

2   Department of State as Currently Organized   65

3   Department of State as Proposed   66

4   Ten Leading U. S. Agricultural Exports, as a
       Percentage of Farm Production, 1974   99

5   Administrative Structure of Export Controls   103

LIST OF ABBREVIATIONS

AMA   American Management Association
CEO   Chief Executive Officer
CIA   Central Intelligence Agency
DOD   Department of Defense
EAO   External Affairs Officer
ECAT   Emergency Committee for American Trade
EEC   European Economic Community
FAS   Foreign Agricultural Service
FSO   Foreign Service Officer
IBF   International Business Fellow
IBM   International Business Machines
IPAC   Industry Policy Advisory Committee
ISAC   Industry Sector Advisory Committee
ITT   International Telephone & Telegraph Company
MFN   Most favored nation
MNB   Multinational businessman
MNC   Multinational corporation
NAM   National Association of Manufacturers
OC   Operating Committee
OECD   Organization for Economic Cooperation and Development
PUWP   Polish United Workers Party
USDA   U. S. Department of Agriculture

The Multinational Businessman and Foreign Policy

1

THE ROLE OF U.S. MULTINATIONAL BUSINESSMEN IN THE CONDUCT OF U.S. FOREIGN POLICY

The objective of this study is to describe and explain the role the U.S. Multinational Businessman (MNB) plays in the conduct and implementation of U.S. foreign policy. In the post-Vietnam, post-Watergate era, the formulation and conduct of U.S. foreign policy is a field where the expertise and experience of U.S. businessmen will be needed. As representatives of multinational corporations (MNCs) the U.S. international business executives influence the outcome of U.S. foreign policy objectives. In the political process, U.S. multinational businessmen fill three corporate roles. As suggested by Nye and Rubin these include a direct role, an unintended direct role, and indirect roles. [1]

Motivation

		Intended	Unintended
Nature	Direct	Private foreign policy makers	Instruments of Influence
of Role	Indirect	Agenda Formulators	

Anthony Sampson suggests that a multinational businessman such as Harold Geneen plays a direct role in the conduct of U.S. foreign policy. [2] As chief executive officer of International Telephone and Telegraph Company (ITT) Geneen's responsibilities include guiding the United States' tenth largest corporation toward a global profit-maximizing strategy. In pursuing this strategy, Harold Geneen has ordered campaign contributions to political parties and lobbying of U.S. government legislators.

1

U.S. multinational businessmen may be used wittingly or
unwittingly by the government to further foreign policy objectives.
The information-gathering potential of U.S. multinational business
executives remains considerable. Cyrus Eaton, for example, was
recruited by the CIA to spy in the Soviet Union but refused.[3] Equally
important has been the use by the CIA of corporate leaders with
government ties to front for its clandestine activities.

U.S. businessmen intentionally and unintentionally act to set
foreign policy priorities. Primarily through their lobbying activities,
multinational executives press for legislative actions by the U.S.
government toward particular host countries. In one case, these
activities included lobbying against restrictive trade amendments,
specifically the Jackson-Vanik Amendment to the Trade Reform
Act of 1973 (H.R. 10710), which affected Soviet-U.S. commercial
exchanges.

Second, U.S. MNBs direct the flow of intraenterprise transactions. These exchanges of capital, raw materials, unfinished
products, technology, and managerial personnel have led toward
increasing intergovernmental cooperation to solve these international problems. For example, from March 17 to March 28,
1975, under the auspices of the UN, the newly-created Commission
on Transnational Corporations held its first session. Established
by the UN Economic and Social Council in Resolution 1913 of
December 5, 1974, the secretary general has requested that the
commission study the impact of multinational corporations on
development and on international relations.

Third, MNBs unintentionally stimulate social group representatives to act against the global strategies of multinational firms.
George Meany, president of the AFL-CIO and organized labor-
spokesman, is one example. Meany feels that international
businesses that employ low-cost foreign workers in plants in Taipei
or Singapore threaten U.S. labor's well-being. Consequently,
President Meany responded by pushing for restrictive trade
legislation such as the Burke-Hartke bill, which would have
empowered the president to restrict the transfer of capital from
the United States; to set import quotas on a category-by-category
and country-by-country basis; to impose strict requirements on
labeling imported products; and to repeal provisions of the tariff
act that permit duty-free reentry of the U.S.-made component of
materials exported from the United States for processing abroad.
Fortunately, the Burke-Hartke bill failed. Realizing that the
proposed restrictions in the act would curtail the United States'
liberalized trade and investment program at home and abroad,
U.S. businessmen responded with an outpouring of public commentary
of the strongest nature on the destructive consequences of such
measures.

ASSUMPTIONS

Contemporary U.S. multinational businessmen and multinational corporations trace their roots to earlier stages in the history of modern capitalism. Nevertheless, the term multinational corporations remains definitionally imprecise.

The most comprehensive definition of multinational corporations will apply in this study. Because the term means different things to different people, the following distinctions propounded by Yair Aharoni, will apply:

1. A world-wide corporation: A corporation registered in several countries, doing business in these countries. The distinct feature of such a corporation is a legal one: it does not incorporate as separate legal bodies in each country under the laws of the various states, but retains one corporate identity. As far as we know, such a corporation does not yet exist. Countries have laws governing alien corporate registration, ownership of land, rights of importing employees, and, above all, tax laws. The definition is needed, therefore, for discussing the reason for the nonexistence of the world-wide corporation, not in explaining its behavior.

2. A multinational cluster: A group of corporations, each created in the country of operation, but all controlled by one headquarters.

3. A multinational corporation: A corporation that controls a multinational cluster. While the former term refers to the cluster as a whole, the latter is reserved for the headquarters. In order to qualify as a multinational corporation, the company should control a multinational cluster in a minimum number of countries. The number of countries must be large enough so that the multinational corporation should be involved in the international field. As a first approximation, we define multinational cluster as consisting of corporations in at least five countries. This, of course, is an arbitrary number. The number of countries may be one vector in describing different multinational corporations.

The multinational corporations should be subdivided according to three additional criteria, namely, the type of operations in which they operate.

According to their operations, corporations can be classified as:

1. Exporters: Companies which control a multinational cluster, the only function of which is to sell and service the products manufactured by the corporation.

2. Importers: Companies which control an international cluster involved in mining operations, whose function is to feed raw materials to the corporation.

3. Transporters: Where the international cluster consists of companies dealing with the transportation of men and goods.

4. Petroleum: The operational problems of the petroleum industry seem to be so unique that a separate classification of these companies is called for.

5. Manufacturers: Companies controlling an international cluster of manufacturing and/or assembly plants.

6. Traders: Companies controlling an international cluster whose main function is trading in various countries (such as Sears Roebuck Co.).

According to their size, corporations can be classified as:

1. Size relative to the host country, measured in terms of total assets controlled or a similar criterion.

2. Size of the multinational cluster relative to the total operations of the corporation.

The first measure is relevant to problems of relations with the host country, and the second relates to commitment.

Corporations can also be classified according to their area of operations:

1. Regional: Confining their multinational cluster to one region, such as Western Europe or Latin America.

2. Multiregional.[4]

Given the definitional parameters, the global activities of these enterprises dramatically influence the pattern of interstate actions among nations of the international political system. Acting as representatives of global corporations, MNBs engage in trans-frontier activities. The most obvious include direct foreign investment, trade, and developmental assistance. To implement these activities, diplomats of sovereign states administer the legislative rules placed upon multinational businessmen and their corporations. In addition to legislative statutes, executive department administrative rulings also act as political constraints upon multinational businessmen's activities within and among national societies. Especially in the arena of U.S. foreign policy, developing a sensitivity to those constraints will strengthen the contribution U.S. MNBs can make in implementing foreign policy goals.

SCOPE OF THE STUDY

U.S. multinational businessmen operate in diverse societies and cultures. In each nation and society, U.S. foreign policy differs from that of the host country. Faced with the prospect of conducting business in so many heterogeneous national environments, the multinational businessman has become politically astute and politically competent. The multinational businessman now finds that he is an international politician. Fundamentally, the channels of U.S. multinational businessmen's influence are both formal and informal, direct and indirect (Table 1.1).

TABLE 1.1

Channels of Corporate Influence

Direct	Indirect
Formal	
Participation in or direct access to key policy-making units	Access to key foreign policy-making units through intermediaries
recruitment	foreign governments
joint ventures	congressmen
contracts	foundations
consultation	nonprofits
lobbying	study groups
	party officials
	trade associations
Informal	
Personal and/or group ties to authoritative and legitimate policy makers	Intermediary nonbusiness groups communicate knowingly or unknowingly the preference of the corporate elite to authoritative and legitimate foreign policy makers.
recruitment	
common socialization	
family ties	
school ties	public opinion
elite club ties	voting patterns

Source: Dennis Ray, "Corporations and American Foreign Relations," in The Multinational Corporation, ed. David H. Blake (The Annals of the American Academy of Political and Social Science, 403, September 1972), p. 85.

Some relevant questions are posed in order to describe the MNB's role and how it influences the conduct of U.S. foreign policy. In reference to East-West trade and investment issues, this study answers a variety of questions. For example, what is the U.S. businessman's input into East-West trade and investment policies? What activities denote U.S. MNBs as political actors? What kinds of programs do MNBs participate in through the U.S. government in effecting foreign economic policies? Do U.S. policy makers believe American MNBs should play a direct role in formulating U.S. foreign policy?

This is a preliminary heuristic study intended to identify the significant factors in the role played by U.S. MNBs in the conduct of U.S. foreign policy in the field of East-West trade and investment. The results are not intended to have sampling generalizability in the statistical sense, although they may well have generalizability in the sense that they identify factors that would be uncovered in a true probability sample. The percentages in Chapter 6 are a description of the sample rather than projections applicable to a relevant population.

This study contains considerable explication of the background concepts derived from social psychology. Secondary source citation from the literature of social psychology has been included so that readers unfamiliar with concepts such as role, position, and status may appreciate the genesis of the concepts used and gain some awareness of their significance in social psychology. In addition, secondary data has been included to describe and analyze the organizations from which the sample of MNCs was drawn.

The purpose and method of this research are cast in terms of social psychological concepts. It should be understood that these concepts, particularly those from role theory, are used in the present study in order to conceptualize the research problem and to provide a language for describing procedures and results. The present research is not in any way intended to test the validity of the social psychological theories from which these concepts are drawn, nor does the descriptive validity of the empirical results of the present study depend upon the validity of these theories.

The central purpose of this research inquiry hinges on producing a set of explanations describing the role U.S. MNBs play in the conduct of U.S. foreign policy. To fulfill this purpose, terms and concepts will be introduced only when needed. In order to place the multinational businessman within the context of his corporation and the U.S. government official in line with his department's outlook, historical and contemporary literature will be taken into account. The aim is to provide a theoretically useful statement of the subject matter. Explicit criteria are used to determine whether the explanations will be useful and significant.

First, the explanations provided should be judged by their organizing effectiveness. As few variables as possible will be used to explain the roles MNBs play in the conduct of U.S. foreign policy. Second, the anecdotes and details provided by MNBs and government officials should be examined in search of unexpected information. Unanticipated insight into what roles MNBs are playing in the conduct of U.S. foreign policy may detail whether the influence of multinational businessmen in this area is increasingly widespread. Last, the outcome of this inquiry should furnish an heuristic contribution. Research questions, questions not previously or otherwise raised, aim at assessing the potential of exploring in greater detail the roles of MNBs in the conduct of U.S. foreign policy.

DEFINITIONS

Multinational Corporations
and Multinational Businessmen

No single complete description adequately defines the terms multinational corporations and multinational businessmen. Jacques G. Maisonrouge, chairman and chief executive officer of the International Business Machines (IBM) World Trade Europe/Middle East/Africa Corporation, uses five basic criteria to define a multinational corporation:

1. It must do business in many countries. I don't think that a company doing business in two or three industrial countries can be considered multinational; it must be in many countries that are in different stages of economic development.

2. It must have foreign subsidiaries with the same R&D, manufacturing, sales, services, and so on, that a true industrial entity has. You can't prepare general managers if you have only a sales organization.

3. There should be nationals running these local companies; they understand the local scene better than anybody else; and this helps promote good citizenship.

4. There must be a multinational headquarters, staffed with people coming from different countries, so one nationality does not dominate the organization too much.

5. There should be multinational stock ownership—the stock must be owned by people in different countries.[5]

Clearly divergent understandings of the multinational enterprise exist. Any analysis of the role MNBs play as representatives of MNCs becomes immediately limited by the definition of the term multinational corporation. As professor of social architecture Dr. Howard V. Perlmutter states:

Part of the difficulty in defining the degree of multinationality comes from the variety of parameters along which a firm doing business overseas can be described. The examples from the four companies argue that (1) no single criterion of multinationality such as ownership or the number of nationals overseas is sufficient, and that (2) external and quantifiable measures such as the percentage of investment overseas or the distribution of equity by nationality are useful but not enough. The more one penetrates into the living reality of an international firm the more one finds it is necessary to give serious weight to the way executives think about doing business around the world. The orientation toward "foreign people, ideas, resources," in headquarters and subsidiaries, and in host and home environments, becomes crucial in estimating the multinationality of a firm.[6]

To provide a solution to this problem, Professor Perlmutter argues:

Three primary attitudes among international executives toward building a multinational enterprise are identifiable. These attitudes can be inferred from the assumptions upon which key product, functional and geographical decisions were made.
    These states of mind or attitudes may be described as ethnocentric (or home-country oriented), polycentric (or host-country oriented) and geocentric (or world-oriented). While they never appear in pure form, they are clearly distinguishable. There is some degree of ethnocentricity, polycentricity, or geocentricity in all firms, but management's analysis does not usually correlate with public pronouncements about the firm's multinationality.[7]

Perlmutter believes that multinationalism may be a state of mind or attitude among international business executives derived from the organization of which they are a part. Moreover, he feels identifiable forces and obstacles exist, pulling MNCs toward and away from geocentrism.

Another long-time student of MNBs and their corporations, Columbia University Professor Richard Eells, defines multinational corporations as quasi sovereigns. He believes if large MNCs act as more or less independent power centers from the nation-state, then the MNCs and their business leaders become quasi sovereigns.

Instead of viewing MNBs and MNCs as quasi sovereigns, other observers like S. Venu find the MNCs to be an instrument of neocolonialism. Venu, economic planning manager with the India Tobacco Company, Ltd., Calcutta, identifies a multinational corporation as an organization that

> fuses equity capital, managerial talent, technology, brand images, marketing ties, distribution networks, etc. which together may constitute a competitive margin over rivals, existing and potential. The world of pure competition does not apply; it is more appropriate to regard it as a model of oligopoly. In 1971, the value of investment abroad by the U S MCs was about $80 thousand million. The European MCs invested $22 thousand million. The Japanese MCs, latest entrants into the field, have invested $4 thousand million. This makes up a total of $106 thousand million out of which approximately $18 thousand million have been sunk in Latin America, Asia and Africa. The balance has been spread out among the developed countries. [8]

Although Venu may believe a multinational businessman acts as an instrument of neocolonialism, former U.S. Under Secretary of State George Ball prefers to call multinational businessmen "cosmopolitans." As representatives of their corporations, like modern-day Marco Polos, multinational executives exercise an ease of mobility into and out of distinct national business environ-ments. MNBs become stateless individuals. They are nationals with allegiance to a multiplicity of foreign governments besides their own.

Value judgments arise as MNCs and MNBs are characterized. This author, like Professor Sidney Rolfe, finds Peter F. Drucker's net assessment of MNCs appropriate. Writing in The Age of Discontinuity, Drucker has said that a world economy needs:

> a producing and distributing institution that is not purely national in its economic operations and points of view. The world economy needs someone who represents its

interests against all the partial and particular interests
of the various members. It needs an institution that has
a genuine self-interest in the welfare of the world economy,
an institution that, in pursuing its own goals, serves the
world economy rather than any one of the individual national
economies. . . . Such an institution . . . we already have
at hand. Its developing during the last 20 years may
well be the most significant event in the world economy,
and the one that, in the long run, will bring the greatest
benefits. This institution is the "multinational
corporation."[9]

Yet in fulfilling the needs of the world economy, conflicts will
arise. U.S. multinational businessmen must confront conflicts
produced by their respective corporations. In order to understand
the role MNBs play in such conflicts, especially as the conflicts
affect U.S. foreign policy objectives, broad-gauged definitions of
multinational, transnational and international organizations will
be used. By definition, a multinational businessman is one who
acts on behalf of a multinational corporation. The goal of
the MNC is to provide goods and/or services across nation-
state territorial boundaries.

The Nature of U.S. Foreign Policy

The foreign policy of a nation-state is the manner in which it
conducts its external affairs with other nation-states. Like the
term multinational corporations, defining the nature of a state's
foreign policy leads to disagreement among international business
executives and politicians. Some, like Professor Richard Falk,
prefer to define foreign policy precisely:

1. a desirable foreign policy—approved means are
used in pursuit of approved ends, with the bases of approval made explicit;
2. an effective foreign policy—means used are
successful in accomplishing ends sought;
3. a popular foreign policy—the main positions
enjoy high levels of public support;
4. a legitimate foreign policy—both the means and
ends of foreign policy are in accord with the Constitution,
including constraints embodied in international law;
5. a populist foreign policy—the means and ends of
foreign policy reflect public participation, influence
filtering up as well as down;

6. an <u>equitable</u> foreign policy—the domestic costs,
burdens, and sacrifices resulting from a given foreign
policy are distributed fairly, i.e., in accordance with
democratic theory. [10]

Often a national political style is used to characterize a nation-
state's foreign policy. <u>Usually either democratic or nondemocratic
political styles apply. The American national political style is one
of self-governing individuals, where the voting public regularly
changes its leaders.</u> By purpose and intent, U.S. government
officials define U.S. foreign policy to be peaceful. U.S. foreign
policy aims at assuring private property, free markets, and profits
for U.S. multinational businessmen.

Diplomats, like Ambassador at Large U. Alexis Johnson,
believe certain characteristics define a nation's foreign policy. In
a speech before the Seattle World Affairs Council, Ambassador
Johnson touched upon the ethnocentric, interdependent, intergovernmental, cooperative, and multilateral characteristics of contemporary
U.S. foreign policy:

First, the basic policy of any country is in the last
analysis going to be determined by that country's
estimate of its own best interests. . .each country
is going to follow those policies that it considers most
likely to benefit itself. . . .

Another characteristic of foreign policy. . . is
the growing degree of interdependence that now exists
among all the peoples and nations of the world. This
means that we no longer can think in terms of foreign
policy as something that exists in isolation from
domestic policy or vice versa. . . .

Related to this question of interdependence is
whether the nation-states of the world are going to be
able to find some way of <u>cooperating</u> together in the use
of the world's shrinking natural resources. . . .

Another characteristic of our foreign relations is
the degree to which we are involved in and concerned with
third-country problems. . .the foreign policy question
existing between us and the Soviet Union involve very
few purely bilateral questions but, rather, arise out
of the relationships each of us has with third countries
and third areas. [11]

Ambassador Johnson suggests MNCs and multinational businessmen
have definitely played a role in the postwar trade explosion and the
development of the international economic system.

The Role of MNCs in the Conduct of U.S. Foreign Policy

Donald M. Kendall, chairman of the board and chief executive officer, Pepsi Co., Inc., and chairman of the Emergency Committee for American Trade (ECAT), recently traced the historical participation of U.S. multinational corporations in the postwar world.

In Kendall's estimation, the role MNCs have played in U.S. foreign policy emerges from considering the huge benefits derived from them. For example, U.S. MNCs stimulate world trade:

> The U.S. imports over 20% of its raw materials. Of the 40 minerals considered essential to U.S. industry, 31 are imported. The United States imports roughly 90% of such commodities as tin, diamonds, cobalt, beryllium, nickel, and manganese, as well as large amounts of mercury, zinc, lead, and iron ore. [12]

Besides providing the U.S. with key strategic materials, a wide range of agricultural imports flow into the U.S. through the multinationals' trade activities. In terms of trade, direct foreign investment, and technology transfer, U.S. MNCs have a decided impact on areas of U.S. foreign policy.

The Role of the U.S. Multinational Businessman in the Conduct of U.S. Foreign Policy

Professor Michael Z. Brooke's and Professor H. Lee Remmers' study of multinational management strategies defines role as

> the activities assumed to be attached to a particular position; relationships that these activities demand are called 'role relationships'. As an example, one of the features of promotion in any organisation is that the higher position is likely to carry with it more roles that have to be played simultaneously, and with them a more complex set of role relationships. [13]

International executives involved in transfrontier operations are involved in a complex web of role relations. At times, when the multinational businessman must perform in different and inconsistent roles, role conflict arises.

In this study, multinational businessmen are those who act in behalf of a multinational corporation. International executives may therefore include chief executive officers (CEOs), heads of personnel,

sales, marketing, finance, or manufacturing divisions, and external
affairs officers (EAOs). This last category includes U.S. government
liaison personnel, corporate information officers, or public affairs
officials. In order to categorize their activities in the conduct of
U.S. foreign policy as entrepreneurial politics, explicit definitions
of both entrepreneur and politics will be used.

Multinational businessmen practice entrepreneurship.
Some think entrepreneurship is the ability to create an ongoing
business activity where none previously existed. Joseph A. Schumpter
provides a suitable definition of entrepreneurship. In his book
Capitalism, Socialism and Democracy, he noted:

> the function of entrepreneurs is to reform or
> revolutionize the pattern of production by exploiting an
> invention or, more generally, an untried technological
> possibility for producing a new commodity or producing
> an old one in a new way, by opening up a new source of
> supply of materials or a new outlet for products, by
> reorganizing an industry and so on. [14]

Professor Richard Henderson summarizes the role of the
entrepreneur, stating,

> The entrepreneur is the counterpart of the pioneer of
> the past. In most cases, he is a loner, although he is
> receptive to the ideas of others. He is extremely self-
> assured, sets high goals for himself, keeps them clearly
> in sight, and is confident that he can attain them. Not
> only does he seek responsibility, he demands it. Risk-
> taking situations do not frighten him because he is
> capable of developing accurate probabilities of success.
> He overestimates neither the assistance of others nor
> the barriers raised by his opponents. . . .
> The entrepreneur's tool box contains an ability to
> focus on problems, identify their true nature, review
> available resources and develop alternative solutions.
> But he is thorough, and what often appears to be an
> instant decision may actually have required hours of
> agonizing thought and review.
> In short, the entrepreneur thinks big. He is a doer:
> he makes things happen. He maximizes the use of his
> creative and innovative talents in the achievement of well-
> defined goals. But, they are his goals--his drives are
> inner-directed. [15]

In terms of this study, the multinational businessman acts like an entrepreneur. Like an entrepreneur, the U. S. multinational business-man sets his goals and purposes and moves firmly in the direction of achieving them.

Our particular interests here are the goals set by MNBs in the field of East-West trade and investment policy. The subject of entrepreneurship has recently received formal study. However entrepreneurial politics, or the politics of multinational businessmen's activities, has not yet received extensive study. Consequently, the need exists to review the role MNBs and U. S. MNCs play in the conduct of trade and investment issues.

As previously described, MNBs appear to be private foreign policy makers, instruments of influence, and agenda formulators. U. S. MNBs represent corporate organizations which today politically challenge the legitimacy, authority, and prerogatives of the nation-state. Professor Joseph Nye of Harvard University believes "the role of the multinational corporation today cannot be understood merely in economic terms, but must be seen in terms of this larger political challenge and response. "[16]

Diplomats, U. S. government officials, and elected represent-atives, traditionally charged with the responsibility for formulating, expressing, and implementing U. S. foreign policy, increasingly find MNBs and MNCs engaged in ordering the priorities of foreign policy issues like trade, direct foreign investment, and technology transfer.

Multinational businessmen's activities derive from the sources of formal and informal political influences which characterize the political process. The sources of political influence may be economic, social, or ideological.
Herein lies our central objective.

ROLE TYPES

The roles U. S. MNBs play in the conduct of U. S. foreign policy approximate one of four types:

Type	Characteristics	Case	Example
1. Formal, direct	Direct access to key policy-making units	Direct MNC payments to U. S. govern-ment officials	Grain scandals
2. Formal, indirect	Access to key foreign policy-	Trade asso-ciation	American Petroleum

Type	Characteristics	Case	Example
	making units through inter-mediaries	lobbyists	Institute's Frank Ikard
3. Informal, direct	Personal and/or group ties to authoritative and legitimate policy makers	Former U. S. government officials employed by MNCs	United Aircraft's Clark MacGregor, former Minnesota congressman
4. Informal, indirect	Intermediary nonbusiness groups communicate knowingly or unknowingly the preferences of the corporate elite to authoritative and legitimate foreign policy makers	Public opinion appeals	Mobil Oil's energy policy advertising campaign

These four generic roles point toward a new partnership between U. S. multinational businessmen and diplomats.

Michael J. Johnson, director of the State Department's Office of Private Cooperation, and Gene E. Bradley, former president of the International Management Association, provide evidence of this new partnership. They find that

American businessmen are learning to act like diplomats and diplomats like businessmen, at a time when neither sector can afford the luxury of going it alone. Government and corporate leaders are learning the crucial interdependence of diplomacy, profits and public affairs programs.

State Department Foreign Service officers are being forced to learn—and are learning—their joint stake with business. In parallel, officials of U. S. international corporations are being forced to learn—and are learning—how to work with government in doing business so as to satisfy both the host community abroad and the share owners back in the U. S. [17]

Evidently, U.S. government officials and MNBs are diligently at work erasing the previous adversary relationship between them.

Former Assistant Secretary of State John Richardson, Jr., clarified four basic roles for U.S. business in the conduct of U.S. foreign affairs:

> First, that American business—quite apart from its economic role—is a major force for good in world affairs. As one example, it is helping to spread world-wide the application of American management techniques and practices.
>
> Second, that this power derives at least in part from the ability of the U.S. international corporation to communicate what is good about Americas's open society. American business, through teaching a pragmatic approach to problem-solving and a democratic approach to the organization of people, is a constructive force favorably affecting the context of our diplomacy.
>
> Third, that American business should put at least as much emphasis abroad as it does here on public affairs programs, civic, cultural, and humanitarian, and that at least as much thought be devoted to the policies affecting its public posture in each country where it does business abroad as such policies receive at home.
>
> Fourth, that the multinational corporation is both the most powerful and the least understood socioeconomic force on the globe today; and it is often misunderstood because—by its nature— it is an instrument of change. [18]

Acting as catalysts for assessments in the conduct of U.S. foreign policy, U.S. multinational businessmen must accept the responsibility implicit in their increasingly evident global impact.

As the number of U.S. MNBs increases, so does their potential collective and individual impact on the conduct of U.S. foreign policy. Under Secretary of State for Political Affairs Joseph J. Sisco agrees. Before the Senate Committee on Foreign Relations, Sisco said: "There is no doubt in our mind that the international political situation will be deeply affected by the way in which we carry out our trade and economic relations."[19] Sisco testified that the emerging issues of U.S. foreign policy clearly engulf the primary areas of interest to U.S. MNBs:

A prosperous multilateral trading relationship is one
of the bases of the political approach that we have
adopted in our relationship with the advanced industrialized nations of the West since World War II. A breakdown in this system would be contrary to our interests.

The recent energy crisis has demonstrated the risks
inherent in nations trying to resolve their problems
unilaterally. The recent Washington Energy Conference
was an initial step toward recognition of the necessity
to deal with multilateral problems on a multilateral
basis.

On the question of trade, our approach has been that
all the major trading nations must act in concert and
in the common interest. We have recognized the necessity
of expanding the flow of trade between the industrialized
and developing countries of the world. One way we seek
to do this is by the extension of a system of generalized
tariff preferences to developing countries.

In short, we seek:

● To reduce trade barriers among the industrialized
countries and to help meet the demands of developing
countries by the expansion of their exports so that
they can proceed with the tasks of economic and social
development;

● To normalize trade relations between the United
States and the Soviet Union and the countries of Eastern
Europe; and

● To enhance global economic relationships on a
multilateral basis, for the benefit of the world's
peoples. [20]

As Sisco implies, the emerging issues of U. S. foreign policy
reflect the broad global concerns of U. S. MNBs. U. S. MNBs will
have a collective and individual impact on the successful implementation
of U. S. foreign policy objectives. If specific U. S. foreign policy goals
are to be met, then MNBs must be willing to participate in activities
that promote reduced trade barriers and normalize trade relations
between the U. S. and the Soviet-bloc economies. As a case study,
the research provides an assessment of a range of MNB activities
in the East-West trade and investment area of U. S. foreign policy.

NOTES

1. Joseph S. Nye, Jr. and Seymour J. Rubin, "The Long Range Political Role of the Multinational Corporation," in Global Companies: The Political Economy of World Business, ed. George W. Ball (Englewood Cliffs, N. J.: Prentice-Hall, Inc., 1975), pp. 126-34

2. Anthony Sampson, The Sovereign State of ITT (New York: Stein and Day, 1973), pp. 314-19.

3. "Eaton Says the CIA Asked Him to be a Spy," The New York Times, June 16, 1975, p. 38.

4. Yair Aharoni, "On the Definition of a Multinational Corporation," in The Multinational Enterprise in Transition, eds. A. Kapoor and Phillip D. Grub (Princeton, N. J.: Darwin Press, 1972), pp. 17-18.

5. Gene E. Bradley and Edward C. Bursk, "Multinationalism and the 29th Day," Harvard Business Review 50, no. 1 (January-February 1972): 39.

6. Howard V. Perlmutter, "The Tortuous Evolution of the Multinational Corporation," in The Multinational Enterprise in Transition, ed. A. Kapoor and Phillip D. Grub (Princeton, N. J.: Darwin Press, 1972), p. 55.

7. Ibid., p. 56.

8. S. Venu, "The Multinationals and Developing Societies: Profile of the Future," Futures 6, no. 2 (April 1974): 133.

9. Peter F. Drucker, The Age of Discontinuity (New York: Harper & Row, 1969) quoted in Sidney Rolfe, The Multinational Corporation (New York: Foreign Policy Association, Inc., 1970), p. 6.

10. Richard Falk et al., "Who Pays for Foreign Policy?" Foreign Policy no. 18 (Spring 1975): 92.

11. U. Alexis Johnson, "Complexities and Accomplishments of U.S. Foreign Policy," Department of State Bulletin 70 (June 10, 1974): 633-34.

12. Donald M. Kendall, "The Need for Multinationals," Columbia Journal of World Business 8, no. 3 (Fall 1973): 105.

13. Michael Z. Brooke and H. Lee Remmers, The Strategy of Multinational Enterprise (London: Longman Group, 1970), p. 125.

14. Karl H. Vesper, "Entrepreneurship, A Fast Emerging Area in Management Studies," Journal of Small Business Management 12, no. 4 (October 1974): 8.

15. Richard Ivan Henderson, "The Best of Two Worlds: The Entrepreneurial Manager," Journal of Small Business Management 12, no. 4 (October 1974): 5.

16. Joseph S. Nye, Jr., "Multinational Corporation in World Politics," Foreign Affairs 53, no. 1 (October 1, 1974): 175.

17. Michael J. Johnson and Gene E. Bradley, " A New Partnership—Businessmen and Diplomats—They're Working Toward the Same Goals," Nations Business 62, no. 9 (September 1974): 74-75.

18. Ibid., p. 76.

19. Joseph J. Sisco, "The U.S. Contribution to a Peaceful World Structure," Department of State Bulletin 70 (April 15, 1974): 384.

20. Ibid., pp. 384-85.

CHAPTER

2

THE RESEARCH FRAMEWORK

The contribution of today's multinational businessman goes beyond his status as a global trader. As a result of structural changes in the world's economy, a political role for MNBs is taking shape. Working as a partner problem solver with counterpart government officials, the MNB's technical knowledge and management efficiency permits him to influence U.S. government policy.

The area of East-West trade and investment are chosen to develop and explain the role American multinational businessmen play in the conduct of U.S. foreign policy. A complex interaction network between MNBs and government officials exists in the U.S. foreign policy field. Three research questions aim at elaborating this network.

First, U.S. government officials were asked what role they believed U.S. MNBs played in the conduct of U.S. foreign policy in the area of East-West trade and investment. Second, as representatives of both food and nonfood multinational corporations, U.S. multinational businessmen were asked to explain the role they fulfilled in the conduct of U.S. foreign policy. A third research question followed: What differences emerge between U.S. government officials and U.S. multinational businessmen over the role the multinational businessmen play in the conduct of foreign policy?

Role theory provides the theoretical framework for answering the research questions. The basis for the research model must be established by examining role theory in some detail.

THE MEANING OF ROLES

Teachers of multinational business find the term role requires specification. Professor of Psychology Hubert Bonner believes,

A role refers to the action performed by an individual who holds a certain status, in anticipation of others' expectations. [1]

One instructor, Y. K. Shetty, thinks,

The term role may be defined as a named social position characterized by a set of (a) personal qualities and (b) activities, the set being norm-atively evaluated to some degree both by those in the situation and others. [2]

Multinational businessmen are the subjects of this study. The multinational differences between international executives determine the role multinational businessmen will play. Dimitris N. Chorafas believes:

It is important to maintain an awareness of the purposes and motivations of executives—both the chief executive who is trying to establish a corporate foothold abroad and the manager who runs a one-man operation in a remote part of the world. These four motivations are vital:
　　　1. Profits. The profit motive was more valid and rewarding in the past than now.
　　　. . . Obviously, profits are a major concern of individuals and organizations, but the belief that they are the only purpose or objective is now considered erroneous and outdated. While the profit motive is a strong stimulus, it is not in itself strong enough to motivate people and companies to undertake the risks, endure the hardships, and tolerate the tiresome work required to be successful in international business.
　　　2. Desire for adventure and challenge. . .
　　　. . . the desire of men to seek adventure and new opportunity, to learn about other cultures, and to meet the challenges of the unknown. . . .
　　　3. Economic contribution. Some international executives see themselves as business representatives

of organizations that contribute to economic wealth.
They understand the role that their companies play in
society, and they want to participate in it. . . .
    4. Social responsibility. In addition to financial
and economic power, executives are able to exercise
another type—power over people. [3]

In short, probing multinational businessmen's motivations makes their
role more clearly understood.

THE NATURE OF ROLE BEHAVIOR

Through the use of prescribed roles, Bonner describes role
behavior. In his opinion,

> The difference, then, between role and role behavior
> is the difference in the function and the act performed
> by the individual: it is the function performed which
> identifies a role and the specific act which distinguishes
> role behavior. . . . "A role behavior," Newcomb asserts,
> is "a motive pattern on the part of a specific individual
> as he takes a role."
>   A role behavior, as we see it is a person's intern-
> alization of his social roles, as he perceives them, in
> such a way that his individual behavior is synchronized
> with the expectancies of other members of his group or
> community. [4]

As Bonner finds, although a multinational businessman's role is a
function of expectations,

> The distinct character of individual roles is normally
> obscured by their strong tendency to form networks of
> interrelated roles. They act in sets or patterns. The
> network conceals their strongly individual nature. The
> sets of patterns themselves, furthermore, tend toward
> individuality; they are characteristic of the person. We
> thus come to identify a person, not by any single or
> isolated role, but by the pattern in which the roles are
> integrated. The set of interrelated roles is the
> person. . . .
>   In knowing the roles he plays and the manner in
> which he enacts them, we know him. [5]

The network of roles enmeshing the multinational businessman can be viewed in terms of reference groups and membership groups.

In clear detail, Bonner discusses the concept of reference groups. He states:

> A reference group is one with which an individual closely identifies himself. The internalization of values of which we have spoken on several occasions, which impels a person to perceive the group's values as his own and to feel that he is acting not under compulsion but on the basis of the group values which he has appropriated, takes place in a reference group.
>
> Reference groups differ from other kinds of groups in the readiness of persons to establish a close identification with them. An individual normally belongs to various groups, to some of which he is only externally or passively related, or to some in which his membership confers practical advantages, or to others largely against his own wishes. A reference group is an association of persons to which he wants to belong and in which he finds satisfactions which other groups do not generally afford him. This group he feels is his group, and the functions which it performs are activities with which he wishes to identify himself. [6]

The importance of reference groups to multinational businessmen has been verified by a study conducted by Professor Reed M. Powell and Associate Professor K. Tim Hostiuck. Powell and Hostiuck sampled 465 middle-level executives in 5 medium to large industrial corporations to determine the business executive's role in politics. According to the Powell and Hostiuck sample, reference groups in the form of peers and superiors exert a powerful force on corporation executives. According to Powell and Hostiuck, executives' political activities and roles are determined by reference and peer group pressure. Powell and Hostiuck emphasized this point in their research, concluding,

> The business executive functions both as an independent citizen and as a representative of his corporation. As he becomes involved in political activities, his behavior has an impact upon both roles.
>
> In this research, it becomes very apparent that two groups primarily determine the extent of the executive's political activism—his peers and his reference group.

> Since the typical executive relates either to his
> peers or to superiors (or both) in the company (as
> opposed to groups outside the firm), it is obvious
> that the corporation can wield considerable
> influence over his political behavior. [7]

If Powell and Hostiuck's findings are correct, then multinational
businessmen's role behavior in the field of U.S. foreign policy
emerges from the activities of the MNBs' reference and membership
groups.

THE ROLE ACTIONS OF U.S. MNBs
IN THE CONDUCT OF FOREIGN POLICY

In some degree, the effects of personality influence the U.S.
MNB's role actions on U.S. foreign policy issues. Brooke and
Remmers believe,

> there are three types of personality among national
> managers: the strategist, the person who is best
> able to grasp the issues and put together a coherent
> planning proposal; the politician, with emphasis on
> the ability to influence other people; and the executive,
> the highly motivated decision-taker. [8]

Although executive role behavior can be analyzed as a function of
personality and social role, this tends to focus entirely on observations
derived from clinical psychology and not from multinational business.

A more practical way to depict MNBs' role actions is to
specify the common denominators of U.S. MNBs' activities as global
administrators. Dimitris Chorafas thinks that the common denominators
that characterize international executives are:

1. An international executive works for an international
company.
2. He has had managerial responsibilities in several
countries.
3. He can integrate the cultural, social, and business customs
and attitudes of people of different nationalities.
4. He is flexible, open-minded, and at ease, regardless of
where he is and what the circumstances are.
5. He is a man who has a broad outlook and self-control, and
does not try to impose his own way of thinking and acting on others.

6. He is able to develop under his command a multinational team, each member of which he trains and motivates to perform in a competent and enthusiastic manner.

7. He is a member of professional societies in several countries and is appreciated by other members of these groups as an equal.

8. He is a man of status who has determination and can stand up and state his case to headquarters when necessary.

9. He appreciates the facts and is able to collect, analyze, and interpret factual data relevant to his job.

These characteristics are a composite of the personal assets possessed—consciously or unconsciously—by executives carrying out international assignments today. 9

These characteristics mean a multinational businessman must act simultaneously in a bundle of task-oriented roles. At any time, a multinational businessman's input into the process of conducting U. S. foreign policy can fall within one or more of these roles:

The initiator-contributor suggests new ideas or different ways of regarding a group problem. This may take the form of proposal of a new goal, a new definition of the problem, a suggested solution, or a new way of mobilizing the group's efforts and skills in problem solving.

The information-seeker asks for elucidation of proposals and for factual or authoriative information pertaining to the problem.

On the other hand, the opinion-seeker is looking not for facts, but for a clarification of the value premises which are related to the problem.

Compared with the information-seeker, the information-giver presents facts, brings his own experience to bear on the problem, or formulates reasonable generalizations.

Unlike the opinion-seeker, the opinion-giver expresses whatever beliefs he thinks might be relevant to the task, particularly his opinion of what the group's values ought to be.

The elaborator concretely spells out or illustrates ideas, presents reasons for suggestions made by the group members, and tries to predict how a suggestion or a proposed solution would work out.

A coordinator clarifies relationships among ideas, tries to pull the ideas together, or attempts to coordinate separate activities into an effective group effort.

An orienter summarizes the discussions and activities of the members in order to enable them to see their position with respect to the group goal, or raises questions concerning the direction which the group discussion is taking.

The evaluator-critic attempts to evaluate the group's achievement in terms of the group task. He may do this by evaluating the logic or feasibility of proposals. [10]

Clearly, numerous aspects of role theory can be used to depict the multinational businessman's role in the conduct of U. S. foreign policy. Unfortunately, research in this field has been neglected.

Presently, only selected articles discuss the issues between U. S. MNBs and politics. Powell and Hostiuck have divided these articles along three lines of inquiry:

1. Why should—or should not—an executive become involved in political activity as an independent citizen?
See James C. Worthy, "The Business Man, Government, and Partisan Politics," in The Business Man in Politics, AMA Management Report, No. 37 (New York: American Management Association, 1959); Reed M. Powell and Dalmas H. Nelson, "Business Executives View the Politician," Business Horizons (October 1968), pp. 41-52; Andrew Hacker and Joel D. Aberbach, "Businessmen in Politics," Law and Contemporary Problems, 27 (Spring 1962), pp. 266-79.

2. What level of political activity is appropriate for an executive?
See Dan H. Fenn, Jr., "Business and Politics," Harvard Business Review (May-June 1959), p. 6 ff.; Stephen A. Greyser, "Business and Politics, 1964," Harvard Business Review, 42 (September-October 1964), pp. 22-24 ff.; and Stephen A. Greyser, "Business and Politics, 1968," Harvard Business Review, 46 (November-December 1968), pp. 4-6 ff.

3. What factors influence an executive's willingness for, or resistance to, involvement in political activity?
See Hacker and Aberbach, "Businessmen in Politics"; Scott D. Walton, American Business and Its Environment (New York: Macmillan Company, 1966), pp. 369-71; Greyser, "Business and Politics, 1968"; Powell and Nelson, "Business Executives View the Politician"; Worthy, "The Business Man, Government and Partisan Politics"; Edwin M. Epstein, The Corporation in American Politics (Englewood Cliffs, N. J.: Prentice-Hall, Inc., 1969), pp. 304-09. [11]

In Powell and Hostiuck's categories, this study is an explanation of the appropriate level of MNBs' political activities in the field of East-West trade and investment policies.

A RESEARCH MODEL

Theoretically, innumerable models about man's nature discuss
U. S. multinational businessmen. For example, MNBs can be pawns
of fate or neutral instruments of forces outside themselves. Others
see the multinational businessman as a rational master. As a master
of his fate, the multinational businessman decides, thinks, and
acts for rational goals such as maximizing returns and minimizing
his losses. Some view MNBs in terms of machine models. The
multinational businessman's motivations become reflex responses to
physical forces in his environment. Darwinists might examine MNBs
as high-order biological animals who behave through instinct and
acquired competitive drives. Other models treat man as a social
product who mirrors his culture. Man might also be an unconscious
being whose basic motives spring from sources deep within himself.
Thus, any model conceptualizing a U. S. multinational businessman's
behavior can never offer a complete picture of his actions.

At this time, constructing a behavioral model of the multinational businessman's activities seems premature. Consequently,
this work is an exploratory study. As Dr. Daniel Katz notes,

> The exploratory study attempts to see what is there
> rather than to predict the relationships that will be
> found. It represents the earlier stage of a science.
> From its findings may come knowledge about important
> relationships between variables, but the more definite
> proof of these relationships comes from hypothesis-
> testing. [12]

An exploratory study may aim at discovering variables or aim at
uncovering relationships.

A Comparative Matrix Model

To find out how U. S. multinational businessmen fill their role
in the conduct of U. S. foreign policy in the area of East-West trade
and investment, MNBs from ten leading U. S. MNCs were interviewed.
The MNBs represented food and nonfood corporations listed in Table
2. 1. This latter category included industrial corporations and defense
corporations. The industrials represented oil and automobile manufacturers. Defense corporations represented the electronics and
aviation sectors. A matrix was constructed from these interviews,
as noted in Table 2. 2.

TABLE 2.1

MNCs[a] Ranked by 1974 Sales[b]

Fortune 500 Sales Rank	MNCs	Kind[c]	Type[d]	1974 Sales ($000)
1	EX	NFI	O	42,061,336
2	GM	NFI	A	31,549,546
3	F	NFI	A	23,620,600
4	T	N	O	23,255,497
5	MO	NFI	O	18,929,033
6	SOC	NFI	O	17,191,186
7	GO	NFI	O	16,458,000
8	GE	NFD	E	13,413,100
9	IBM	NFI	E	12,675,292
10	ITT	NFI	E	11,154,401
11	C	NFI	A	10,971,416
15	WE	NFD	E	7,381,728
29	W-LTV	IM	f	4,768,010
30	E	F	f	4,615,715
31	RCA	NFI	E	4,594,300
33	K	F	f	4,471,427
35	RI	NFD	Av	4,408,500
39	B	NFD	Av	3,730,667
42	BF	F	f	3,541,216
45	A(G)	IM	f	3,458,336
46	UA	NFD	Av	3,321,106
47	BC	F	f	3,264,502
49	L	NFD	Av	3,222,000
54	McD	NFD	Av	3,075,036
55	R-P	F	f	3,073,210
58	GF	F	f	2,986,692
74	CC	F	fB	2,522,150
76	TRW	NFD	E	2,486,022
84	UB	F	f	2,230,106
98	GD	NFD	Av	1,968,416
100	R	NFD	Av	1,928,855

[a]The multinational corporations listed by abbreviations are: (One of the top three grain companies, that is, Cargil, Continental Grains, Cook Industries, also participated but did not wish to be singled out from among these firms.)

TABLE 2. 1

Explanatory Notes, Continued

Armour (Greyhound)	A (G)	Kraftco	K
Beatrice Foods	BF	Lockheed	L
Boeing	B	McDonnell-Douglas	McD
Borden Company	BC	Mobil Oil	MO
Chrysler	C	Ralston Purina	R-P
Coca-Cola, Inc.	CC	Raytheon	R
Esmark	E	RCA	RCA
Exxon	EX	Rockwell International	RI
Ford	F	Standard Oil of Cali-	
General Dynamics	GD	fornia	SOC
General Electric	GE	Texaco	T
General Foods	GF	TRW, Inc.	TRW
General Motors	GM	United Aircraft	UA
Gulf Oil	GO	United Brands	UB
IBM	IBM	Western Electric	WE
ITT	ITT	Wilson & Co (LTV)	W-LTV

[b]Sales include service and rental revenues, but exclude
dividends, interest, and other nonoperating revenues. All companies
on the list must have derived more than 50 percent of their sales
from manufacturing and/or mining. Sales of subsidiaries are included
when they are consolidated; sales from discontinued operations are
included when these figures are published. All figures are for the
year ending December 31, 1974, unless otherwise noted. Sales
figures do not include excise taxes collected by the manufacturer, and
so the figures for some corporations—most of which sell gasoline,
liquor, or tobacco—may be lower than those published by the corporations themselves. See Bro Uttal, Fortune, May 1975, p. 230.

[c]Nonfood - industrial   NFI
   Nonfood - defense   NFD
   Industrial - multiservice   IM
   Food   F

[d]Auto   A   Food   f
   Aviation   Av   Food, beverage fB
   Electronics   E   Oil   O

TABLE 2.2

MNBs' Perspective—MNBs' Roles in the Conduct of
U.S. Foreign Policy

Roles	Formal, Direct	Formal, Indirect	Informal, Direct	Informal, Indirect	No Role
MNBs from Food MNCs					X
MNBs from Nonfood MNCs Industrials Oil	X	X			X
Autos	X	X			
Defense Electronics	X				
Aviation	X	X		X	
Total (n=10)	4	3	0	1	2

Source: Jeffrey M. Brookstone, "Entrepreneurial Politics: The
Role of American Multinational Businessmen in the Conduct of U.S.
Foreign Policy; A Case Study of East-West Trade and Investment
Policies," Ph.D. dissertation, George Washington University, 1976.

Unlike hypothesis-testing research, the objective of this study
is to discover relationships. The main relationships involve U.S.
MNBs and the U.S. foreign policy-making process. As an exploratory
study, this is an investigation where there are no specific predictions
of relationships based upon theoretical derivations. While the
researcher has hypotheses in mind, these are not precisely formulated.
Instead, U.S. multinational businessmen's behavior is described in
terms of episodes. In the case of East-West trade and investment
policies, changes in these policies are brought about by what MNBs do
in a selected number of individual cases.

As noted in Chapter 1, the primary goal of this book centers on
the role MNBs play in the conduct of U.S. foreign policy, especially
in the East-West trade and investment areas. Four types of role
behavior were designated: (1) formal, direct; (2) formal, indirect;

(3) informal, direct; and (4) informal, indirect. This research explores the political activity of MNBs in relationship to the key variable, the power structure of the U.S. government. The roles MNBs play in the conduct of U.S. foreign policy are examined and compared from the contrasting perspectives of U.S. government officials and U.S. MNBs. This task is accomplished through a comparative matrix model.

To find out what role U.S. government officials thought U.S. MNBs filled in the conduct of U.S. foreign policy in the area of East-West trade and investment, bureaucrats from five U.S. government agencies were interviewed. The bureaucrats represented the Departments of State, Commerce, Defense, Treasury, and Agriculture. A matrix was constructed from these interviews, as noted in Table 2.3.

TABLE 2.3

Bureaucratic Perspective—MNBs' Roles in
the Conduct of U.S. Foreign Policy

Roles	Formal, Direct	Formal, Indirect	Informal, Direct	Informal, Indirect	No Role
U.S. officials from the Department of					
State	XXX	X		X	
Commerce	XXXX	X	X		X
Defense	XXX				
Treasury	XX	X			
Agriculture	X	X	XX	X	
Executive office	X	X			
Total (n=25)	14	5	3	2	1

Source: Data compiled by the author (see Table 2.2)

By comparing the results of Tables 2.2 and 2.3, the role behavior of U.S. MNBs is contrasted with what U.S. government officials find that role behavior to be.

Criteria for the Sample

Sampling involves the selection from the whole population of a smaller group to be investigated. Two separate populations were sampled. One was composed of MNBs

First, on the basis of their sales, a sample was chosen of the leading Fortune 500 industrial companies. All top 11 companies were selected, except General Electric. [13] General Electric was picked up in the list of top ten Defense Department Research and Development Companies. [14] The remaining corporations were selected from among the top ten food corporations. [15]

One privately owned corporation, Hughes Aircraft, was eliminated from the sample. One of the top three grain corporations was added. Overall, the sampled corporations could be considered publicly owned. As Table 2.4 indicates, a stratified sample of America's largest corporations provided a cross section of American multinational business spokesmen:

TABLE 2.4

MNB Interview Sample

Company Type	Number of MNCs	Number MNBs Interviewed	Percent of Sample
Auto	3	2	20
Aviation	7	3	30
Electronic	5	1	10
Food	10	1	10
Oil	5	3	30
Total	30	10	100

Source: Data compiled by the author (see Table 2.2)

Multinational businessmen were grouped on the basis of their age (Table 2.5), present job experience (Table 2.6), educational level (Table 2.7), and job responsibilities (Table 2.8).

TABLE 2.5

MNBs by Age Group

Age Group	Number MNBs Interviewed	Percent of Sample
Under 25	0	0
25–34	0	0
35–43	0	0
44–50	4	40
51–55	2	20
55+	4	40
Total	10	100

Source: Data compiled by the author (see Table 2.2)

TABLE 2.6

MNBs and Present Job Experience

Years in Position	Number MNBs Interviewed	Percent of Sample
5 yrs.+	7	70
1–5 yrs.	2	20
6 mon.–1 yr.	0	0
6 mon. or less	1	10
Mode Experience: > 5 yrs.		

Source: Data compiled by the author (see Table 2.2)

TABLE 2.7

MNBs and Education

Level	Number MNBs Interviewed	Percent of Sample
High school	0	0
College graduate*	2	—
Graduate school	8	80
Other	2*	20

*MNBs with B.S. degrees also had specialized nondegree graduate training.

Source: Data compiled by the author (see Table 2.2)

TABLE 2.8

MNBs and Job Responsibilities

Type	Number MNBs Interviewed	Percent of Sample
External government relations	6	60
Formulation East-West trade	5	50
Administration East-West trade	7	70
Communicate East-West trade	8	80

Source: Data compiled by the author (see Table 2.2)

The second sampled population was composed of U.S. government officials or bureaucrats. Bureaucrats were selected from five departments which have major intergovernmental units handling East-West trade and investment problems (see Table 2.9).

TABLE 2.9

U.S. Government Personnel in East-West Trade Field

Department	Intergovernmental Unit	Number Interviewed		
State	Bureau of Economics and Business Affairs	2		
	Bureau European/Eastern European Affairs	1		
	Office East-West Trade	1	State	
	Office of Private Organizations	1	Subtotal:	5
Commerce	Office Deputy Assistant Secretary for East-West Trade	1		
	Office East-West Trade Development	2		
	Office East-West Trade Analysis	2		
	Office of Export Administration	1	Commerce	
	USSR Affairs Division	1	Subtotal:	7
Treasury	Office of Assistant Secretary of International Affairs	2	Treasury	
	Office of International Affairs	1	Subtotal:	3
Defense	Defense Supply Assistance Agency	0		
	Defense Supply Agency	0		
	Office Deputy Assistant Secretary, International Economic Affairs	3	Defense Subtotal:	3
Agriculture	Foreign Agricultural Service	4	Agriculture	
	Economic Research Service	1	Subtotal:	5
Other: The Executive Office	Office of Special Trade Representative	1		
	Council on International Economic Policy	1	Other Subtotal:	2
	Total U.S. government officials interviewed:			25

Source: Data compiled by the author (see Table 2.2)

U. S. government officials were chosen on the basis of their age (Table 2. 10), present job experience (Table 2. 11), GS rating (Table 2. 12), educational level (Table 2. 13), and job responsibilities (Table 2. 14).

TABLE 2. 10

Bureaucrats by Age Group

Age Group	Number Bureaucrats Interviewed	Percent of Sample	
Under 25	0	0	
25 – 34	7	28	
35 – 43	3	12	
44 – 50	2	8	
51 – 55	3	12	32
55 +	10	40	
Total	25	100	

Source: Data compiled by the author (see Table 2. 2)

TABLE 2. 11

Bureaucrats and Present Job Experience

Years in Position	Number Bureaucrats Interviewed	Percent of Sample
5 years +	6	24
1 - 5 years	9	36
6 months - 1 year	7	28
6 months or less	3	12
Mode experience: 1 - 5 years		100

Source: Data compiled by the author (see Table 2. 2)

TABLE 2.12

Bureaucrats by GS Rating

GS Rating	Number Bureaucrats Interviewed	Percent of Sample
1 - 8	0	0
9 - 12	4	16
13 - 15	15	60
16 +	6	24
Total	25	100

Source: Data compiled by the author (see Table 2.2)

TABLE 2.13

Bureaucrats and Education

Level	Number Bureaucrats Interviewed	Percent of Sample
High school	0	–
College graduate	4	16
Graduate school: law, business, engineering	21	84
Total	25	100

Source: Data compiled by the author (see Table 2.2)

TABLE 2.14

Bureaucrats and Job Responsibilities

Type	Number Bureaucrats Interviewed	Percent of Sample
External government relations	6	24
Formulation East-West trade	11	44
Administration East-West trade	20	80
Communicate East-West trade	21	84

Source: Data compiled by the author (see Table 2.2)

Interviewing and Data Collection

Due to time constraints, a complete case study of the role U.S. MNBs play in the conduct of U.S. foreign policy would be impossible. The writer therefore limited himself to a single field of U.S. foreign policy, East-West trade and investment. This permitted analysis of one set of political relationships between U.S. government policy makers and U.S. MNBs.

A structured interview schedule was utilized. The interviews undertaken for this study depict the roles American multinational businessmen fill in the conduct of U.S. East-West trade and investment policies. The perspective of a U.S. MNB or government official will be a function of his total informational knowledge. In an exploratory study of U.S. MNBs, a limited number of their insights into the conduct of U.S. foreign policy can be presented.

Interviews suffer from three common drawbacks. One drawback is the involvement of the researcher in the data he is reporting and the resulting likelihood of bias. If they choose, respondents can withhold or distort information in personal interviews. Second, the scope of an interview is limited because the respondent may be unable to provide certain types of information. This factor, plus a third, memory bias, means a respondent may provide inaccurate information due to inadequate recall ability. Despite these drawbacks, the interview can be a powerful instrument for social research.

To minimize the drawbacks inherent in the interview technique, certain procedural safeguards were adopted. First, a structured interview schedule was developed. Utilizing a mixture of open-end, two-way, and multiple choice questions, the respondent's feelings on the roles MNBs fill in the conduct of U.S. foreign policy were closely probed. Second, where permissible, the interviews were recorded on cassette tapes to insure recall of anecdotal detail. Because the interviews were precoded, the researcher could mark the interview schedule and transcribe on paper answers given during the question and answer exchanges.

To prevent interviewer personal bias and control the quality of the data, the researcher established additional controls. First, pretest interviews were conducted with both MNBs and U.S. government officials. After evaluations of the pretest interviews, an amended interview schedule was utilized. Second, in some U.S. government departments, two top bureaucrats were interviewed within one week with the second bureaucrat not being advised that the first had been interviewed. Third, MNBs and former U.S. government officials outside the sample were interviewed.

With a theoretical framework in mind, additional topics on the role of U. S. multinational businessmen in the conduct of U. S. foreign policy can now be presented. The first one focuses on the making of U. S. foreign policy and multinational businessmen's input into East-West trade and investment policies.

NOTES

1. Hubert Bonner, Group Dynamics: Principles and Applications (New York: Ronald Press Company, 1959), p. 375.

2. Y. K. Shetty, "International Manager: A Role Profile," Management International Review 11, no. 4-5 (1971): 19.

3. Dimitris N. Chorafas, Developing the International Executive (New York: American Management Association, Inc., 1967), pp. 16-17.

4. Bonner, op. cit., p. 382.

5. Ibid., pp. 384-85.

6. Ibid., pp. 395-96.

7. Reed M. Powell and K. Tim Hostiuck, "The Business Executive's Role in Politics," Business Horizons 15, no. 4 (August 1972): 56.

8. Michael Z. Brooke and H. Lee Remmers, The Multinational Company in Europe (London: Longman Group Ltd., 1972), p. 63.

9. Chorafas, op. cit., p. 20.

10. Bonner, op. cit., pp. 390-91.

11. Powell and Hostiuck, op. cit., p. 49.

12. Daniel Katz, "Field Studies," in Research Methods in the Behavioral Sciences, eds. Leon Festinger and Daniel Katz (New York: Holt, Rinehart and Winston, 1953), p. 74.

13. Bro Uttal, "The Fortune Directory of the 500 Largest Industrial Corporations, " Fortune 91, no. 5 (May 1975): 208-35.

14. "Top 500 DOD Research and Development Contractors," Aviation Week and Space Technology 102, no. 5 (February 3, 1975): 50-55.

15. Carl R. Havighorst, "U. S. Super-Corporations in Food: FE Analyzes the Top 75," Food Engineering, no. 1 (January 1975): 45-55.

3

U.S. MNBs' INPUT INTO EAST-WEST TRADE AND INVESTMENT POLICIES

AN OVERVIEW OF CONTEMPORARY U.S. POLICY

Secretary of State Henry A. Kissinger considers nation-state interdependence the central theme of present-day foreign policy. Kissinger has stated,

> We must recognize that the common interest is the only valid test of the national interest. It is the common interest, and thus in the interest of each nation. . . That growing economic interdependence lift all nations and not drag them down together. [1]

In the field of U.S. relations with the Soviet Union and the Eastern European countries, nation-state interdependence has yet to emerge. Dr. George F. Kennan, former U.S. ambassador to the Soviet Union, notes:

> If today a shadow of doubt continues to hang over the durability of the dominant Soviet position in Central and Eastern Europe, it flows not from Western policy but from the attitudes and reactions of the respective peoples themselves. That Soviet hegemony over this region involves serious strains has been made pain- fully evident, at one time or another, in every one of the countries except Bulgaria. To some extent, the strains have been eased here and there by relaxations in the rigor of Soviet control; but basically, the situation continues to be in many ways delicate and difficult,

and there is a tendency for new forms of strain to
arise as older ones are removed. [2]

As Kennan implies, U. S. foreign policies towards communist
Eastern European nation-states should not be explained through
monocausal statements about Soviet totalitarian control over them.
Competing explanations of U. S. foreign policies appear
in journalistic accounts and the academic literature. Generally,
these competing explanations are strategic, bureaucratic, democratic,
or economic ones. Too often, critics of one explanation discount as
falsehoods alternative explanations of U. S. foreign policy. However,
the theme of nation-state interdependence in U. S. foreign policy
places an emphasis upon the explanatory process of national economic
management.
Professor George Modelski concluded that the advantages of a
national system of economic management include:

(1) capacity to deal with problems of development in
the perspective of the entire nation; (2) ability to
correct imbalances in development and to reduce
income inequalities and cultural disparities; (3)
greater responsiveness to the entire national
constituency; and (4) maximization of national
advantage toward outsiders. [3]

On the other hand, the weakness of the nation-state system cannot
be overlooked. According to Modelski,

The weaknesses of the nation-state system are considerable, too, and are most obvious when considered
in global perspective:
(1) The system functions best in a situation of
autarchy or self-sufficiency. But in conditions of
rising interdependence it has no provision for total-
system or global coordination; it allows or allocates
no resources for the performance of global functions.
(2) Nation-states as presently constituted vary
greatly in size and capacity. Few provide a basis for
effective economic coordination; many, in fact, only
malfunction. Those most in need of coordinated action
are those least able to produce it.
(3) Nation-states tend to subordinate economic or
welfare considerations to the pursuit of governmental
interests, to national security and prestige, and, if
unchecked, to expansion. [4]

In short, the diversity and heterogeneity of the Eastern European nation-states limits the making of generalizations about U.S. trade and investment policies in Eastern Europe.

Many believe the activities of U.S. MNBs effectively blur the distinction between domestic and U.S. foreign policies. In view of the transfrontier diffusion of technology, Eugene B. Skolnikoff finds that

> Interdependence is a significant causative factor in this phenomenon as is the ease with which domestic developments can be publicized and related to foreign policies. Further, the expansion of the subject matter of international relations has brought more elements of society and government into direct participation in foreign affairs. This expansion is facilitated to the extent that the primacy of the Department of State among government agencies in foreign policy making has been seriously eroded. Television has had a substantial impact in making foreign policy a subject of intense and immediate debate and thus has made it easier to relate foreign and domestic issues within the country. [5]

Besides the mass media impact, in searching for profitable business opportunities, U.S. MNCs act to achieve a position of economic integration within host countries. In sum, the making of U.S. foreign policy reflects the need to promote international political cooperation among nation-states. Global cooperation among nations facilitates the international economic activities of U.S. MNCs and their multinational executives.

POLICY MAKING IN FOREIGN AFFAIRS

In the past three decades, the process of formulating and executing U.S. foreign policy has changed dramatically. The president still retains constitutional responsibility for foreign policy. However, many new actors, such as the National Security Council, the Office of Management and Budget and other parts of the Executive Office combine with numerous departments and government agencies to provide a noticeable input into the making of U.S. foreign policy. Some departments, such as defense and agriculture, have sizeable political and financial resources, which they use to influence the public and Congress. Nongovernmental agencies, such as trade associations and unions also play significant lobbying roles, particularly on economic, technical, trade, and investment policies. Moreover, the Department of State must contend with the Congress.

As in the past, because of its constitutional grant of
appropriation, appointment, investigation, treaty ratification, and
war-making powers, today's Congress continues to influence the
formulation and execution of U.S. foreign policy. However,
congressional officials find they make only partial decisions. Partial
decisions result because

> the decision makers themselves approach issues with
> limited information, with prior biases and with external
> pressures that are in turn based on partial information
> and special interests. [6]

Consequently, U.S. foreign policies emerge from a disorderly and
complex policy-making process. The process accounts for some
confusion over what is the precise nature of U.S. trade and
investment policy in Eastern Europe.

Historically, the post World War II foreign policy of the
United States was containment. U.S. actions, including the
Berlin Airlift, the Marshall Plan, the defense of South Korea, Taiwan's
membership to the United Nations Security Council, and U.S. support
of South Vietnam were all parts of a grand strategy to control and/or
roll back the internationalist expansionist tendencies of communism.
Communism was viewed as a monolithic, Moscow-dominated movement. Eastern bloc trade was taboo. By 1960, following Mao Tse-
Tung's disenchantment with Khrushchev, the Chinese Communists
became the more unpredictable adversary of U.S. foreign policy. The
Soviet-U.S. relationship became one of competitive coexistence.
Throughout the 1960s and early 1970s, the United States' Vietnam
engagement received harsh criticism from Peking and Moscow.
The 1968 election of Richard M. Nixon foretold a fundamental U.S.
foreign policy shift away from containment and toward detente.

DETENTE: THE PROBLEMS AND PROSPECTS

The Meaning of Detente

Detente is an emotional concept. Its meaning varies widely,
depending upon one's viewpoint and motives. The official U.S.
government position was developed by its chief architect, Secretary
of State Kissinger. To Kissinger, detente means linking progress in
trade relations directly with the settlement of specific international
political issues:

> It was only after the 1972 summit that the President
> determined that trade could reasonably be expanded.

By that time we were on the way to a Viet-Nam settlement. Berlin had been the subject of a major formal agreement, the first SALT agreements had been completed, a set of Principles setting standards for U. S. - Soviet relations had been signed at the summit, a series of bilateral cooperation agreements in a wide field of activities had been signed and were in process of implementation. [7]

By timing the granting of required export credits and licenses to Eastern European countries, implementation of detente could proceed along administration-approved lines.

U. S. MNBs define detente in terms of long-term trade and investment profit opportunities. The U. S. business community believes detente suggests a general normalization of economic relations with the Soviet Union and Eastern European communist countries. Additionally, normalization provides an opportunity to compete for lucrative Eastern European markets. As Table 3. 1 indicates, with the removal of barriers to East-West trade between 1972 and 1973, U. S. imports to and exports from Eastern bloc countries rose quickly. This was especially true of U. S. import sales to Czechoslovakia, East Germany, Poland, Romania, and the Soviet Union.

The Nature of U. S. -Soviet Relations

Eastern European trade and investment programs form only one aspect of overall U. S. -Soviet relations. Dr. Marshall D. Shulman has distinguished seven planes in the relationship between the Soviet Union and the U. S. These include: (1) strategic-military competition, (2) conventional military competition, (3) political competition, (4) trade and economic competition, (5) ideological conflict, (6) the plane of cultural relations, and (7) functional cooperation. [8] In Shulman's opinion, Soviet-U. S. commercial relations, while increasingly evident, nevertheless remain on a small scale. He notes,

U. S. -Soviet trade has increased from a little over $200 million in 1971 to $642 million in 1972; for 1973, trade is running at an annual rate of $1. 4 billion, of which almost $800 million is in agricultural products. Currently, Soviet imports from the United States exceed its exports by more than five times. Of greater significance is the determined Soviet effort to seek long-term, large-scale Western investment in the development of Soviet natural resources in Siberia and other areas. [9]

TABLE 3.1

1973 Trade Results with Western Industrialized Nations
(millions of U.S. dollars)

	Albania Imports	Albania Exports	Bulgaria Imports	Bulgaria Exports	Czechoslovakia Imports	Czechoslovakia Exports	East Germany Imports	East Germany Exports	Hungary Imports	Hungary Exports	Poland Imports	Poland Exports	Romania Imports	Romania Exports	Soviet Union Imports	Soviet Union Exports
Austria: 1973	0.4	2.3	33.5	19.2	103.0	114.7	72.6	53.5	133.8	131.5	130.0	88.6	63.7	53.4	92.2	136.3
1972	.8	1.5	23.8	15.8	71.3	86.6	44.0	38.7	93.6	85.5	78.9	68.6	51.2	32.3	94.2	111.4
Belgium: 1973	.3	.1	14.1	8.3	41.0	40.2	47.0	51.1	21.9	16.9	124.0	79.8	41.1	13.5	212.5	178.3
1972			11.5	7.1	39.2	34.5	25.0	43.8	20.3	15.4	55.9	45.2	21.5	11.2	88.1	103.8
Canada: 1973	.3		.5	1.8	9.9	42.9	3.1	5.7	7.4	13.1	45.1	29.5	12.9	14.8	291.9	22.9
1972	12.3	4.2	.4	1.7	9.6	34.3	9.6	4.4	5.1	11.6	31.2	21.5	13.3	11.9	285.9	15.3
Denmark: 1973	.1		3.9	4.8	21.7	35.2	31.8	31.5	24.3	23.1	61.4	69.2	13.8	9.3	35.0	87.4
1972	.1		2.9	3.2	17.1	24.8	24.8	22.5	16.3	12.5	41.4	50.6	11.3	5.8	26.8	36.7
Finland: 1973	.01	.01	5.7	3.5	14.2	21.0	23.4	22.3	12.0	19.2	34.8	66.2	7.1	13.6	438.2	513.0
1972	.02	.01	3.3	4.5	14.2	14.6	15.8	19.2	9.1	12.0	28.1	47.7	13.4	16.6	365.0	385.1
France: 1973	2.9	1.0	39.6	27.4	79.7	80.9	82.1	107.3	95.2	68.9	268.5	167.4	168.6	123.3	577.3	433.8
1972	.8	.8	28.6	22.7	63.9	62.7	139.3	82.6	90.5	50.3	151.9	117.9	135.3	88.8	341.5	295.9
West Germany: 1973	2.2	1.6	157.5	106.0	567.7	377.6	1,163.8	1,064.7	398.0	317.7	1,005.7	463.6	444.6	326.6	1,184.0	761.5
1972	4.0	.8	98.1	75.7	384.5	271.9	1,172.5	948.7	265.0	207.0	455.3	309.6	300.0	252.2	720.0	434.7
Italy: 1973	9.9	9.9	67.2	89.3	86.0	132.7	48.0	57.0	113.4	270.7	186.7	271.3	130.0	207.1	351.5	441.5
1972	8.7	7.6	59.8	62.7	80.2	90.7	29.9	50.9	102.9	205.2	127.2	207.7	102.2	162.4	268.4	325.0
Japan: 1973	.1	.3	35.8	18.0	39.0	27.9	38.4	15.8	10.7	14.6	83.5	71.0	71.0	27.1	485.7	1,075.2
1972			21.1	13.4	15.0	13.2	47.7	12.1	11.6	9.8	89.1	40.0	48.0	21.2	504.8	593.2
Netherlands:[1] 1973	.6	.2	12.9	8.0	41.6	46.1	92.4	48.4	39.2	34.6	83.9	55.2	33.0	38.1	59.2	84.6
1972	1.2		12.0	8.0	51.6	48.3	79.3	53.7	45.1	43.6	63.5	47.2	22.3	27.6	54.8	79.2
Norway: 1973	.01		3.6	1.3	15.8	24.7	29.4	31.2	11.4	11.3	49.0	62.3	9.2	2.0	22.0	47.2
1972			9.9	3.5	9.7	15.6	18.0	27.1	6.7	7.8	27.8	51.6	2.8	2.0	19.7	28.1
Spain: 1973	.1	.03	10.2	13.0	11.2	19.2	14.5	9.0	9.1	8.7	35.5	59.5	17.4	33.4	116.3	51.1
1972	.1		9.0	6.8	9.9	11.7	17.3	3.7	9.8	22.2	31.5	38.5	12.9	20.5	84.6	29.6
Sweden: 1973	.7	.3	18.7	4.9	46.2	47.8	90.5	75.2	37.5	35.2	176.2	106.9	38.4	31.2	96.0	208.4
1972	.9		10.0	8.7	33.5	34.1	61.6	48.1	25.7	26.4	87.1	69.9	27.7	17.3	69.2	159.4
Switzerland: 1973	1.3	.1	19.3	7.9	63.5	56.5	56.7	19.8	50.0	49.6	89.6	28.8	52.4	20.8	238.0	64.4
1972	1.3		17.1	6.5	44.6	45.1	28.6	15.4	33.2	30.1	54.3	20.8	36.7	12.5	227.4	30.4
United Kingdom: 1973		.1	32.5	22.5	66.5	95.9	34.3	64.2	65.1	41.2	270.8	237.3	83.0	78.0	1,190.3	880.4
1972			23.5	17.1	59.1	80.9	37.5	54.2	57.6	29.5	187.7	178.1	96.7	63.7	550.3	611.8
United States: 1973	.2	.3	6.5	4.5	72.1	35.1	27.9	10.6	33.0	16.4	360.6	182.0	116.6	55.9	238.0	216.1
1972	.1		3.3	2.6	47.3	28.1	14.9	10.6	22.6	12.5	111.8	139.2	69.4	31.4	227.4	95.9
Yugoslavia:[1] 1973	7.2	10.2	44.4	45.4	126.6	187.2	81.8	143.8	53.2	80.4	126.1	120.9	73.6	105.3	408.6	495.8
1972	6.5	5.4	36.3	42.1	128.2	150.4	84.4	100.2	54.2	70.9	100.4	82.1	55.4	63.0	329.4	283.0

*January through September.

Source: Senate staff report, U.S. Trade and Investment in the Soviet Union and Eastern Europe, Committee print, 93rd Cong., 2nd sess., Washington, D.C.: Government Printing Office, 1974, pp. 8–9.

45

Just as future U. S. -Soviet investment prospects seem likely, functional cooperation between the two countries has begun. For example,

> In the course of two summit meetings, the Soviet Union
> and the United States have signed more than ten bilateral
> agreements. . . . Many of these provide for Joint
> Commissions to implement the agreements. . . . Taken
> together with the agreements related to security,
> commerce, taxation, maritime affairs and cultural
> relations, these forms of cooperation constitute the
> "web of interdependency" which the two countries
> are consciously weaving. [10]

In essence, the easing of U. S. -Soviet tensions suggests the opening of Eastern European trade channels as a by-product of detente.

In the areas of East-West trade and investment, the Soviet leadership is emphasizing cooperative relationships with the U. S. and her Eastern European allies. To overcome weaknesses in her economy, the Soviet Union has sought advanced Western technology and capital. In addition, after recognizing the viability of the European Economic Community, the Soviet Union is now furthering commercial ties between the EEC and its Eastern European counterpart, Comecon.

The Politics of East-West Trade and Investment

Traditionally, U. S. government trade and investment policy in Eastern Europe imposes a constraint on U. S. MNBs. On many goods and services, export controls effectively closed Eastern European markets to U. S. multinational executives. However, with the dawn of detente, U. S. commercial relations and U. S. MNBs' trade and investment activities have taken on an important foreign policy priority. Through executive agreements, President Nixon and Soviet Communist Party General Secretary Leonid Brezhnev proposed Soviet-U. S. relations of mutual economic advantage.

In the field of commerce, most of the Nixon-Brezhnev accords sought the expansion of Soviet-U. S. economic ties. For example,

> The political momentum developed at the 1972 summit
> resulted in a formula to settle the stubborn problem of
> our lend-lease account, which led, in turn, to the ex-
> tension of Export-Import Bank credits and guarantees
> needed for sustained trade expansion with the U. S. S. R.

We have concluded a maritime agreement under
which 40 ports in each country have been opened to
prompt access by merchant and research vessels of the
other. We have signed a carefully balanced trade
agreement designed to take into account the structural
asymmetrics of trade between a market and a state
trading economy. In 1973, we concluded a tax treaty
and signed protocols opening commercial offices in our
respective countries and establishing a joint trade and
economic council to foster the development of United
States-Soviet trade. [11]

Thus, trade became a key element in the U.S. overall policy of
detente with the Soviet Union. Simultaneously, a congressional
legislative drive began. This drive stressed using the incentive
of U.S. trade as a means to achieve political goals with the Soviets.
Lewis Bowden, former acting deputy assistant secretary
of commerce for East-West trade, discussed with congressional
members the tenuous position U.S. MNBs must accept when dealing
with the Soviets. Bowden believes that

we must disabuse ourselves of the notion that the U.S.
has technology and products so distinctly superior to
those of our competitors that we can extract major
political concessions from the Soviets in exchange
for our willingness to trade with them.
They do have alternatives. . . . If we attempt to
achieve political objectives through our trade policy
that cannot be accepted by the ruling Soviet hierarchy,
the movement toward economic detente with the U.S.
could be stalemated and the opportunities to influence
their policies through peaceful negotiations would be
significantly reduced. [12]

Congressional representatives brushed aside Bowden's warning.
Through the Jackson-Vanik Amendment to the Trade Reform Act of
1973, H.R. 10710, Congress emphasized the link between U.S.
trade and domestic, Soviet political reforms.
The goal of the Jackson-Vanik Amendment was to force
specific changes in the Soviet's discriminatory policies toward
religious minority groups. Clearly, U.S. MNBs' opportunities
to enlarge Eastern bloc trade took secondary consideration to the
Jackson-Vanik Amendment. Senator Jackson insisted that 60,000
emigration visas a year be set as the minimum standard of initial
compliance for the Soviet Union. Presently,

Adding Soviet Jewish emigration to other countries
besides Israel would make the total for 1974 near
20,000. The 1973 total to Israel alone was 33,461.
In 1972 it was 31,329. [13]

In the U.S. business community, many think the Jackson-Vanik
Amendment is a forecast of future trade and investment statutes.
It is legislation purposefully designed as an impediment to potential
East-West trade.

U.S. MNBs' INPUT INTO EAST-WEST
TRADE AND INVESTMENT POLICIES

U.S. Government Policy Coordination for East-West
Trade and Investment

In the last two years, a significant effort was undertaken to
coordinate efficiently East-West trade policy. As noted in Figure 1,
an intragovernmental group, the East-West Trade Policy Committee,
has monitored the changing nature of U.S. trade and investment
with the Soviet Union and her Eastern European allies.

Historically, the East-West Trade Policy Committee found that
on a year-to-year basis, U.S.-Soviet trade has not been large.
From 1966 to 1973, total U.S. exports to the USSR were just over
$2.28 billion while imports for the period approached $639.8 million.
As Table 3.2 indicates, since 1969, U.S. exports to the Soviet Union
have continued to rise. Similarly, as Table 3.3 indicates, U.S.
exports to the Eastern European countries are slowly increasing.

East-West Investment

As Table 3.4 indicates, most U.S. direct investment abroad
has occurred in other industrialized countries, as in Canada, European,
or Latin American nations. Consequently, present-day U.S. direct
investment in the Soviet Union and Eastern European countries
remains negligible. In the past two years, at least two U.S. corporations have taken the initiative in East-West investment. One,
Boeing Aircraft, signed protocol agreements with Soviet officials
following discussions on cooperative projects in the field of
civil aviation:

Negotiations included the possible construction of
Boeing of an airplane manufacturing facility in the
Soviet Union. The Soviet news agency TASS reported

FIGURE 1

Structure of East-West Policy Making in U.S. Government*

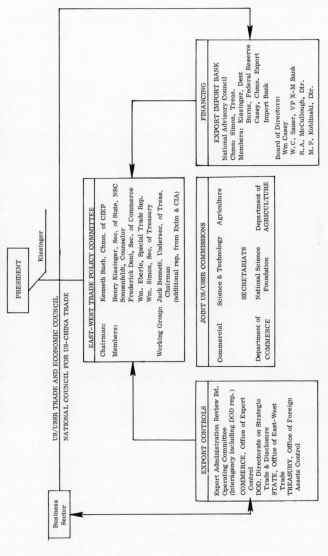

*As of July 1974

Source: Senate staff report, U.S. Trade and Investment in the Soviet Union and Eastern Europe, Committee print, 93rd Cong., 2nd sess., Washington, D.C.: Government Printing Office, 1974, p. 13.

TABLE 3.2

U.S.-USSR Trade, by Major Commodity Groups, 1966–1973
(thousands of U.S. dollars)

	1966	1967	1968	1969	1970	1971	1972	1973	1966-73
U.S. EXPORTS									
1. Food, beverages, tobacco	145	257	910	1,204	2,284	16,900	370,656	842,656	1,235,012
2. Crude materials	23,233	32,130	18,015	22,054	31,896	26,601	71,456	72,796	298,181
3. Mineral fuels and related material		196	15	342	775	33		19	1,380
4. Oils, fats, and waxes	7,599						1,700	5,586	14,585
5. Manufactures classified by material	1,203	1,690	685	7,725	8,775	10,472	10,253	34,653	75,457
6. Chemicals	4,883	13,125	20,636	27,536	24,689	38,098	20,976	16,785	166,728
7. Electric machinery and apparatus	444	1,587	2,681	3,855	3,560	6,250	7,228	14,474	40,079
8. Nonelectric machinery	3,427	9,264	11,853	35,907	37,424	53,957	53,481	181,853	387,166
9. Transport equipment	164	653	463	1,808	3,336	2,696	1,353	7,980	18,453
10. Miscellaneous manufactured articles	331	1,172	1,916	4,073	5,293	6,618	9,163	9,132	37,698
11. Other domestic exports	194	203	228	254	190	276	706	1,698	3,749
12. Reexports	57	32	70	785	172	111	130	2,671	4,028
Total	41,680	60,309	57,472	105,543	118,395	162,012	547,102	1,190,303	2,282,816
U.S. IMPORTS									
1. Food, beverages, tobacco	767	891	406	674	619	263	713	868	5,201
2. Crude materials	16,377	14,410	15,505	14,470	18,313	15,654	17,963	11,228	123,920
3. Mineral fuels and related material			2	1,177	2,807	652	7,464	76,416	88,516
4. Oils, fats, and waxes		1,984				1	1	12	2,002
5. Manufactures classified by material	30,251	21,725	39,969	32,067	46,443	35,086	63,666	118,283	387,490
6. Chemicals	1,387	1,125	1,017	1,312	912	1,062	1,250	2,307	10,372
7. Electric machinery and apparatus				5	17	73	396	76	567
8. Nonelectric machinery	1	105	183	84	49	45	39	42	558
9. Transport equipment				2		1	3	39	59
10. Miscellaneous manufactured articles	459	557	1,071	1,592	2,615	3,044	3,199	4,140	16,677
11. Other imports	163	132	65	89	446	1,344	819	1,381	4,439
Total	49,405	40,929	58,218	51,473	72,223	57,225	95,536	214,792	639,801

Source: House Committee on Foreign Affairs, Detente Hearings, 93rd Cong., 2nd sess., Washington, D.C., Government Printing Office, p. 248.

TABLE 3.3

U. S. Exports to and Imports from Communist Countries: 1967 to 1973, and January to September 1974
(thousands of U. S. dollars)

Country	1967	1968	1969	1970	1971	1972	1973	January to September 1974
Exports, including reexports [1]								
Total	195,260	215,024	249,288	353,645	384,242	882,690	2,490,711	1,774,092
U.S.S.R.	60,308	57,728	105,547	118,712	162,013	542,214	1,194,651	415,643
East Europe	134,950	157,296	143,739	234,932	222,212	276,909	606,416	595,635
Albania	56	8	18	4	16	217	221	445
Bulgaria	4,219	4,036	4,645	15,294	4,353	3,543	6,474	7,619
Czechoslovakia	19,155	13,956	14,363	22,512	38,726	49,993	72,087	30,865
German Democratic Republic	26,329	29,047	32,373	32,545	25,441	17,473	28,025	15,275
Hungary	7,570	11,194	7,252	28,263	27,873	22,613	32,956	47,801
Poland	60,825	82,375	52,694	69,915	73,271	113,642	350,039	292,317
Romania	16,796	16,680	32,394	66,399	52,532	69,428	116,614	201,313
People's Republic of China	[2]1					[3]63,537	689,596	762,811
Mongolia	1		2	1	2	19	31	3
North Korea								
North Vietnam					[4]15	[4]11	[4]17	
General imports								
Total	179,814	200,755	197,819	226,514	228,522	353,957	592,940	750,967
U.S.S.R.	41,167	58,453	51,504	72,312	57,225	95,536	220,072	264,952
East Europe	136,057	139,976	143,953	153,463	165,792	225,034	306,152	396,813
Albania	335	283	396	151	279	470	488	244
Bulgaria	2,814	3,731	1,598	2,431	2,614	2,872	4,458	7,259
Czechoslovakia	26,241	23,756	24,063	23,892	23,597	27,972	35,162	34,127
German Democratic Republic	5,647	5,934	8,018	9,394	10,136	10,336	10,516	11,432
Hungary	3,884	3,848	4,077	6,224	7,751	12,725	16,736	52,412
Poland	90,960	96,871	97,835	97,946	107,641	139,172	182,856	182,840
Romania	6,176	5,553	7,966	13,425	13,774	31,487	55,936	108,499
People's Republic of China	181	(5)	24	1	[6]4,922	32,422	64,874	87,748
Mongolia	2,409	2,326	2,338	738	583	965	1,842	1,454
North Korea								
North Vietnam								

[1] In this table, the term "reexport" refers to an export from the U.S. of foreign origin goods. Elsewhere in this report "reexport" refers to the shipment of U.S. origin goods from one foreign country to another.
[2] Figures shown include printed matter under general license and shipments to diplomatic missions of foreign countries.
[3] This figure does not include shipments of about $550,000 from Guam, which are not considered to be U.S. exports in Bureau of Census statistics.
[4] Data are for surgical supplies shipped under validated license.
[5] Less than $500.
[6] No imports were received directly; all came by way of third countries.

Note.—Exports are shown by area of destination. Imports are credited to the area in which the merchandise was originally produced, not necessarily the area from which purchases and shipments were made. General imports represent merchandise entered immediately upon arrival into merchandising of consumption channels plus commodities entered into bonded customs warehouses for storage.
U.S. exports to North Korea were embargoed in July 1950, and those to People's Republic of China, Manchuria, and Outer Mongolia were embargoed the following December. On July 26, 1954, exports to North Vietnam were embargoed. In February 1972, a list of commodities eligible for export to the People's Republic of China under general license, parallel to the general license list for Eastern European countries, was published and other commodities were made eligible for consideration for validated licenses.
Imports from North Korea and the People's Republic of China were placed under license control on December 17, 1950 through the Foreign Assets Control Regulations of the Treasury Department. On May 5, 1964, license control of imports from North Vietnam was added to these regulations. In June 1971, a general license was established authorizing importation without restriction of goods from the People's Republic of China. Under the regulations in effect prior to June 10, 1971, the importation of goods from the People's Republic of China was prohibited without license by the Treasury Department and it was generally contrary to the policy of that agency to license such imports, except goods for noncommercial purposes which, effective December 22, 1969, were permitted by general license. Some items of People's Republic of China origin, however, continued to appear in the statistical records of U.S. imports. In U.S. import statistics, goods originating in the People's Republic of China are credited to that country regardless of the last country from which they were shipped.

Source: U. S., Department of Commerce, Domestic and International Business Administration, Bureau of East-West Trade, Export Administration Report, Fourth Quarter 1974, 110th Report on U. S. Export Controls to the President and the Congress, p. 36.

TABLE 3.4

U. S. Direct Investments Abroad, by Area and Major Industry, 1960–71
(millions of U. S. dollars)

	Book values							Value of total assets		Value of net fixed assets	
	1960	1962	1964	1966	1968	1970	1971 [1]	1966	1970 [2]	1966	1970 [2]
All areas (total)	31,865	37,276	44,480	54,799	64,983	78,178	86,001	124,792	203,076	43,937	69,012
Manufacturing	11,051	13,250	16,935	22,078	26,414	32,261	35,475	49,156	78,000	19,502	30,915
Petroleum	10,810	12,725	14,328	16,222	18,887	21,714	24,258	27,280	43,871	15,130	22,696
Other	10,004	11,301	13,757	16,499	19,682	24,203	26,268	48,356	81,205	9,305	15,401
Canada (total)	11,179	12,133	13,855	17,017	19,535	22,790	24,030	30,345	42,634	11,689	18,723
Manufacturing	4,827	5,312	6,198	7,692	8,568	10,059	10,537	12,587	16,514	4,957	6,945
Petroleum	2,664	2,875	3,196	3,608	4,094	4,807	5,134	5,369	8,355	3,707	6,531
Other	3,688	3,946	4,461	5,717	6,873	7,924	8,359	12,389	17,765	3,025	5,247
Europe (total)	6,691	8,930	12,129	16,233	19,407	24,516	27,621	49,959	80,367	15,070	22,517
Manufacturing	3,804	4,883	6,587	8,879	10,797	13,707	15,538	22,894	37,263	8,874	13,913
Petroleum	1,763	2,385	3,122	4,003	4,635	5,466	6,202	8,701	13,360	4,530	5,976
Other	1,124	1,662	2,420	3,351	3,975	5,343	5,881	18,364	29,744	1,666	2,628
Latin America (total)	8,365	9,524	10,254	11,498	13,101	14,760	15,763	20,081	23,996	7,621	8,643
Manufacturing	1,521	1,944	2,507	3,318	4,005	4,621	4,998	7,342	10,719	2,806	4,075
Petroleum	3,122	3,642	3,589	3,475	3,680	3,938	4,194	4,002	4,323	2,521	2,408
Other	3,722	3,938	4,158	4,705	5,416	6,201	6,571	8,737	8,954	2,294	2,160
Other areas (total)	5,630	6,689	8,242	10,051	12,940	16,112	18,587	24,407	56,079	9,557	19,129
Manufacturing	899	1,111	1,329	2,189	3,044	3,874	4,402	6,333	13,504	2,865	5,982
Petroleum	3,261	3,823	4,421	5,136	6,478	7,503	8,728	9,208	17,833	4,372	7,781
Other	1,470	1,755	2,492	2,726	3,418	4,735	5,457	8,866	24,742	2,320	5,366

[1] Preliminary.
[2] Estimated from sample data.

Source: Book values from U.S. Department of Commerce, "Survey of Current Business," asset figures from data supplied to the U.S. Tariff Commission by U.S. Department of Commerce, Bureau of Economic Analysis, International Investment Division.

Source: U.S., Congress, Senate, Committee on Finance, Subcommittee on International Trade, The Multinational Corporation and the World Economy, 93rd Cong., 1st sess., Washington, D. C.: Government Printing Office, 1973, p. 45.

that the protocol could lead to cooperation in the design
and construction of new aircraft. Boeing spokesmen
emphasized that the protocol merely formalized discussions which had been going on for years and that no
specific agreements had been reached. The American
firm could not proceed with any specific projects
without U. S. Government approval. [14]

The second U. S. MNC, Occidental Petroleum, is led by Armand
Hammer. He is a U. S. executive who once dealt with Lenin.
Under Hammer's guidance, Occidental Petroleum has signed a

. . . 20-year $20 billion agreement involving the
construction of major chemical fertilizer plants in
the Soviet Union in exchange for Soviet shipments to
the United States of ammonia, urea, and potash. [15]

Since 1973, numerous other U. S. MNCs have signed cooperative
agreements with the Soviet Union. These corporations include Coca-
Cola, Kaiser Industries, PPG Industries, Inc. , Phillip Morris, Inc. ,
General Dynamics Corporation, General Motors, Control Data
Corporation, Pepsico, and General Electric. These cooperative
agreements emphasize prospective joint venture investment projects
between U. S. MNCs and Soviet state agencies. Some of these MNCs
are also exploring Eastern European investment programs. Presently,
however, in Bulgaria and other Eastern bloc countries, constitutional
bars to private ownership of the means of production prohibit foreign
capital investment. Several examples illustrate this fact:
In Czechoslovakia,

Direct foreign investment. . . continues to be forbidden
by law and there is no prospect of a change. Cooperative
ventures ("industrial cooperation") permitted with
Western firms do not involve any element of foreign
investment; sales of technology and licensing arrangements do not usually involve provision of management services or technology on a continuing basis.

A rare exception to this is services to be provided
for the Intercontinental Hotel presently under construction in Prague. Thus, although Czechoslovakia
takes a positive approach to commercial contacts with
American firms, the question of investment does not
apply. [16]

A similar situation prevails in Hungary. So far,

> the Hungarian Government has not yet given the necessary
> approval to the establishment of any joint company with
> foreign equity investment, and present indications are
> that, if approval is forthcoming at all, it will be granted
> only on a most exceptional basis. There are no other
> possibilities for foreign investment in Hungary.
> Hungary has been active in encouraging cooperation
> agreements, and so far over 300 such agreements have
> been signed between Hungarian enterprises and Western
> firms. In general, these have involved production-sharing
> agreements and licensing-repurchase agreements.
> Examples of successful cooperation arrangements in-
> volving American corporations have been the construction
> of luxury hotels and the implementation of American-
> inspired closed-production farming methods in Hungarian
> agriculture. [17]

In Poland, the Polish government strongly encourages
industrial cooperation agreements between Western companies and
Polish enterprises. Since 1972,

> serious consideration has been given to a fundamental
> change in Polish policy which would permit and encourage
> the establishment of mixed-capital joint ventures.
> Presumably, such a change would permit Western
> partners to hold a minority share in a joint-manufacturing
> venture, with provisions for participation in manage-
> ment. . . . Western firms are free to submit proposals
> for various forms of industrial-cooperation agreements.
> Each proposal is to be examined on its own merits. [18]

Since early 1971, Romania has encouraged foreign investment
through joint ventures. Passed to encourage Western investment
in the fields of tourism, scientific and technological research,
agriculture and industry, enabling legislation sets out the primary
requirements for jointly owned Romanian companies. These
requirements are:

> (1) the Romanian share of the registered capital must
> be at least 51%, (2) the Romanian Government guarantees
> the repatriation of profits and capital to the foreign
> partner, (3) production for export is a requirement,
> (4) raw materials and other supplies may be purchased

locally or imported, (5) up to two representatives
from the Romanian Ministry of Finance must belong
to the Board of Managing Directors of the company's
accounting division, and (6) profits of the joint company are taxed 30% annually. [19]

In Romania, although OPIC programs have been operating since
April 1973, no coverage has yet been granted.

Of all the Eastern European countries, Yugoslavia has most
actively sought Western direct private investment. In 1967,
Yugoslavia became the first socialist country to pass a joint venture
law. This law

permits a foreign partner to acquire 49% equity in
a joint enterprise, with 51% remaining in the hands of
the Yugoslav partner. Earnings may be repatriated on
the basis of the firm's export earnings and foreign
exchange retention quota. Since its inception, various
amendments to the law have been enacted to make investments more attractive. These include measures to ease
profit transfer, to eliminate re-investment require-
ment tax incentives, and to guarantee that no subsequent
legislation can worsen the conditions which govern an
existing joint venture. [20]

Additional statutory provisions place Yugoslavia at the forefront of
East-West investment. For example,

The signing of an agreement with OPIC on January 18,
1973, providing political risk insurance, increased U.S.
business interest in direct investment in Yugoslavia.
As of January 15, 1974, 14 U.S. joint ventures had been
registered, amounting to more than $25 million in U.S.
investment, most of which has occurred since the OPIC
signing. [21]

Presently, the Soviet Union permits no foreign equity
or management participation. Instead of turnkey plants, the
Soviets prefer production sharing. That is,

The participating foreign firms or consortium provides specialized machinery, equipment, and expertise,
while the Soviet contribution includes labor and local
procurement of raw materials and intermediate
inputs. [22]

In the hopes of future Western investments, three U.S. banks
as well as thirteen U.S. firms maintain permanently accredited
representational offices in Moscow.

The Role of American MNBs in the Field of East-West Trade and Investment

For a variety of reasons, U.S. MNBs may oppose economic
detente with the Soviets and Eastern European countries. Lewis
Bowden finds the opposition emerging from three general categories:

> Those who would rule out any significant economic relation-
> ships with the U.S.S.R. on the grounds that "trade makes
> them stronger."
> Those who would trade with the U.S.S.R. provided
> that the U.S.S.R. makes certain political concessions.
> Those who are willing to trade, but feel that we
> are in some way subsidizing the Soviets--that we are
> engaged in some sort of "giveaway" program and that
> the terms of trade should be "tougher."[23]

Unlike the opposition, other U.S. MNBs support economic
detente. These U.S. multinational executives give primary
consideration to the long-term profitability of Eastern bloc trade.
However, it is too simplistic to view U.S. MNBs as either
opponents or supporters of East-West policies. U.S. MNBs' inputs
in the East-West trade and investment areas should center on the
substitution of commercial arrangements for emigration reforms
as the means for cementing Soviet-U.S. economic detente.

Donald Kendall, president of Pepsico, Inc., and chairman
of the U.S.-USSR Trade and Economic Council, believes sales
opportunities, not emigration restrictions, offer the optimum
results for achieving detente. A similar concern is felt by
Dr. Lester C. Hogan, vice chairman of the Board, Fairchild
Camera and Instrument Corporation. Hogan believes,

> Eastern Europe is the last sizeable, commercial
> market which has not been tapped by the U.S. semi-
> conductor industry or its Japanese or European
> competitors. There is no other comparable region
> possessing the potentially huge consumer demand for
> products utilizing semiconductors which has not already
> been penetrated by Western semiconductor firms. This
> market, we estimate, will provide billions of dollars of
> semiconductor sales over the next decade.[24]

However, the Soviets rejected the provisions of the 1973 Trade Bill.
Soviet rejection resulted from the fact that the concessions were
interlocked with the granting of most-favored-nation (MFN) status.
The Soviets viewed this development as U. S. tampering and
intercession with the domestic relations of the Soviet Union.

In future Soviet-U. S. commercial relations, a recurrence
of the Jackson-Vanik Amendment's provisions will produce fruitless
results. Replacing emigration problems with commercial problems
suggests a more realistic means of promoting political and economic
detente. Already U. S. businessmen have voiced a number of
specific complaints. These could serve as discussion points for
Soviet-U. S. agreements on MFN and Lend-Lease issues. For
example, U. S. businessmen in Moscow find that

1. Housing and office space are difficult to obtain
and expensive.

2. The Soviet government will issue only one multiple entry
visa to a firm. If a firm is represented by more than one individual,
exits and reentries by the other members of the firm can be difficult
and time-consuming.

3. Because there is a lack of office-trained secretarial
personnel in the Soviet Union, a U. S. firm will often train Russian
employees at its own expense. This process often involves a
period of training in the United States. After such training, it is
not unusual for Soviet state enterprises to raid the U. S. firm for
its newly trained Russian employees.

4. The most serious deterrent to the U. S. businessman in
the Soviet Union is his lack of access to relevant information. A
glaring example of this problem is the refusal of Soviet officials
to permit U. S. business representatives to inspect sites where the
companies are being asked to participate in construction projects. [25]

Although formal procedural difficulties in the area of Soviet-American
trade relations should be negotiated, the U. S. multinational businessmen's inputs in this area encompass a wider role.

In a fundamental sense, the U. S. MNB's role encompasses
U. S. policy in the conduct of American foreign commercial relations.
In the field of East-West trade and investment policy, the impact of
U. S. MNBs is three-fold. First, they act to lead and sustain a
particular foreign policy issue. The MNB's effectiveness fluctuates
with the varying magnitudes of importance on a given issue. For
example, Donald Kendall's leadership of ECAT provided a substantial
policy input into the 1973 Trade Reform Act. Other lobbying groups
such as the American Jewish Committee counterbalanced ECAT's
effects by direct political appeals supporting the Jackson-Vanik
Amendment. However, even under U. S. multinational businessmen's

leadership, reconciling East-West trade arguments proves difficult. The arguments U.S. MNBs win with politicians hinge on a second crucial input: information.

U.S. MNBs represent an independent base of information. Their technical expertise and political policy views emerge from the distinct contributions of their corporations. By utilizing the MNC's resources, U.S. MNBs generate additional perspectives on East-West trade and investment issues. Especially in international marketing, the strength of corporate information is tied to objectivity and factual presentation. For example, one aviation executive related how he frequently discusses antitrust considerations with Department of Justice officials in the company of his business competitors. Lockheed, McDonnell-Douglas, and Boeing multinational executives argue that Export-Import Bank credits can be justified only if sales of wide-bodied 707s to Eastern bloc countries can be based on the competitive, technical edge one competitor offers against another. 26 However, together the three corporations think Eastern European governments should not be permitted to negotiate sales in a "leap frog" manner. Leap frog negotiations blunt inter-MNC competitiveness. The result is competitive price reductions benefiting the Eastern European buyers instead of the U.S. sellers. In short, U.S. MNBs should emphasize their own MNCs' informational input. This input serves as the standard for evaluating the effectiveness of U.S. foreign policies in the East-West trade and investment fields.

Providing informational input and exerting policy leadership does not preclude a third input of U.S. MNBs. The role behavior of U.S. multinational executives requires special interest group identification. In East-West trade and investment matters, U.S. MNBs interact among themselves through a profusion of trade associates. Groups such as the National Machine Tool Builders Association, the Aerospace Industries Association, and the Marine Cargo Insurance Industry are mobilized to provide forums in which U.S. MNBs may organize and speak to national audiences. Trade associations and interest groups collect information and synthesize MNBs' concerns. This input involves development of alternative policy strategies. These strategies are legitimate counterproposals to congressional, executive and bureaucratic initiatives of the U.S. government. U.S. MNBs refuse to leave the world of foreign policy substance strictly to U.S. government policy makers. Through trade associations, U.S. MNBs gain an input as political actors.

As political actors, U.S. MNBs play devil's advocates. The multinational businessmen's input provides creative criticism leading to abandonment or modification of unsuitable East-West trade and investment programs. Through the input of U.S. MNBs, additions or deletions of statutory language clarify the intention of Eastern

European trade legislation. In the Eastern European trade and
export licensing areas, the operational expertise of U. S. MNBs is
particularly crucial to implementing the promises of Soviet-American
economic detente.

To optimally utilize the full input of U. S. MNBs in the East-
West trade and investment field, cooperative relationships between
U. S. government officials and U. S. MNBs must be achieved. In the
past, U. S. MNBs and government officials have not always worked
as partners. Instead, bureaucrats and MNBs have worked at cross
purposes to each other. Bureaucrats and MNBs have operated
within their separate and distinct fields. Yet the increasingly
intense commercial relations between the U. S. and her trade
partners raise expectations of global interdependence among nation-
states. Nevertheless, before hopes of national interdependence are
fulfilled, diplomats and multinational executives must understand
two key developments. The first is the place of the U. S. multinational enterprise in the present international political system.
Second, U. S. MNBs must be viewed as global political actors. An
understanding of the attributes of U. S. MNBs and those of U. S.
diplomats provides an insight into the changing nature of East-West
commercial intercourse.

NOTES

1. Henry A. Kissinger, "An Age of Interdependence: Common
Disaster or Community," Department of State Bulletin 71, no. 1842
(October 14, 1974): 499.

2. George F. Kennan, "After the Cold War. American
Foreign Policy in the 1970's," Foreign Affairs 51, no. 1
(October 1972): 217.

3. George Modelski, "Multinational Business: A Global
Perspective," International Studies Quarterly 16, no. 4 (December
1972): 424.

4. Ibid.

5. Eugene B. Skolnikoff, "Science and Technology: The
Implications for International Institutions," International Organization
25 (Fall 1971): 761.

6. Eugene B. Skolnikoff, Scinece, Technology and American
Foreign Policy (Cambridge, Mass.: MIT Press, 1967), p. 14.

7. U. S., Congress, Senate, Committee on Foreign Relations,
U. S. Trade and Investment in the Soviet Union and Eastern Europe,
The Role of Multinational Corporations, a staff report, 93d Cong.,
2nd sess., Washington, D. C.: U. S. Government Printing Office,
December 29, 1974, p. 6.

8. Marshall D. Shulman, "Toward A Western Philosophy of Coexistence," Foreign Affairs (October 1973) reprinted in House Committee on Foreign Affairs, Detente Hearings, pp. 542-44.

9. House Committee on Foreign Affairs, Detente Hearings, p. 543.

10. Ibid., p. 543.

11. Ibid., p. 48.

12. Ibid., p. 242.

13. Ibid., p. 571.

14. U.S., Congress, House, Committee on Foreign Affairs, Detente: Prospects for Increased Trade with Warsaw Pact Countries, Report of a Special Study Mission to the Soviet Union and Eastern Europe, August 22 to September 8, 1974, Washington, D.C.: U.S. Government Printing Office, October 24, 1974, p. 43.

15. Ibid.

16. Chamber of Commerce of the United States, The Climate for Investment Abroad, (Washington, D.C.: Chamber of Commerce, September 1974), p. 46.

17. Ibid., pp. 46-47.

18. Ibid., p. 47.

19. Ibid., p. 48.

20. Ibid., p. 49.

21. Ibid., p. 50.

22. Ibid., p. 49.

23. House Committee on Foreign Affairs, Detente Hearings, op. cit., p. 239.

24. Senate staff report, U.S. Trade and Investment in the Soviet Union and Eastern Europe, p. 10.

25. House Committee on Foreign Affairs, Detente: Prospects for Increased Trade with Warsaw Pact Countries, op. cit., pp. 17-18.

26. U.S. General Accounting Office, Export of U.S.-Manufactured Aircraft—Financing and Competiveness, Washington, D.C.: Government Printing Office, no. B-114823, March 12, 1975, pp. 1-49.

4

U.S. MULTINATIONAL BUSINESSMEN AS POLITICAL ACTORS

U. S. MULTINATIONAL ENTERPRISES IN THE INTERNATIONAL POLITICAL SYSTEM

Historically, the international political system has been equated with a finite number of nation-states. Nation-state interactions included external economic and commercial relations between states. However, in response to the multinational corporation, the nature of the international system is undergoing change. MNCs demonstrate an increasing potential for nongovernmental international activity. This activity may challenge the authority and legitimacy of the nation-state. Indeed, one must view the role behavior of U. S. MNBs as spokesmen for their MNCs in the context of the present international political system.

As director of Ohio State University's program on Transnational Intellectual Cooperation in the Policy Sciences, Dr. Chadwick F. Alger has directed comprehensive evaluative studies on the nature of the international political system. He finds that six basic changes have occured since World War II:

1. The number of independent nations in the system has greatly increased, primarily through the acquisition of independence by former colonial territories of European nations in Africa and Asia.

2. Regional integration is spreading among the older nations, particularly among the developed nations of Europe.

3. The richer and poorer nations are developing greater group identity and developing institutions in which they can pursue their common concerns. The richer nations use the Organization for Economic Cooperation and Development (OECD) for developing common strategy in their relations with the poorer nations.

4. Global functional organizations, such as the World Meteorological Organization, International Civil Aviation Organization, and World Health Organization have grown modestly in importance, and there is increasing interest in the development of new global functional activities for the sea, environment, and outer space.

5. Nongovernmental ties between citizens of different nations have grown tremendously. For example, the number of nongovernmental international organizations grew from 1, 000 in 1956 to 2, 300 in 1970.

6. Particularly in the larger, older nations—but not exclusively—subnational units (urban, regional, and ethnic) rather than the nation unit, seem more relevant than in the recent past to the solution of some major social problems. [1]

Although only a partial list, our interest focuses on Alger's claim that nongovernmental ties between citizens of different nations have grown tremendously. These ties include U. S. MNBs representing global companies like IBM.

Jacques G. Maisonrouge, chairman and chief executive officer of the IBM World Trade Europe/Middle East/Africa Corporation, believes IBM is one of the most typical of these global companies. Maisonrouge notes,

In addition to IBM's extensive operations and facilities in the United States:
● we operate in 126 countries overseas with some 125, 000 employees;
● we do business in 30 languages, in more than 100 currencies;
● we have 23 plants in 13 countries;
● we have 8 development laboratories in as many countries;
● and we have a very healthy offshore growth rate, going from $51 million in gross income in 1950 to $5. 14 billion in 1973. In fact, since 1970 our overseas business has accounted for more than half the corporation's net income. [2]

While IBM employs over 125, 000 people outside the United States and operates more than eleven scientific centers in eight countries, according to Maisonrouge, IBM's full impact in the international political system centers upon the reduction of military, economic conflicts between nations. IBM's multinational executives make this contribution in at least four ways:

1. The movement of people from country to country that it fosters broadens their experience, outlook, and understanding of others.

2. The flow of capital around the world that it generates increases the interdependence of economies and the commonality of national interests.

3. Through the transfer of technology, it reduces the economic and social gaps between countries.

4. And the infusion of modern management techniques for which it is responsible helps close the "management gap," thereby increasing knowledge of how to maximize the use of resources.[3]

Despite this contribution, the rapid growth of global firms like IBM cannot help but generate tension within the international political system.[4]

Professor Jack N. Behrman recently analyzed the clash of national interests with MNCs. In the Eastern European countries, threats to state socialism are heightened by contact with MNCs. Behrman, a former assistant secretary of commerce, pinpoints the problem. He writes:

> Economically, the governments which do not believe
> that the free market is the best coordinator of the
> economic life of the country consider that the enter-
> prise may upset its own plans for the economy and,
> at times, thwart the government's objectives. Politically,
> host governments fear that the nation will become sub-
> servient to the power of the multinational enterprise.
> Moreover, they see the multinational enterprise as a
> potential channel for economic and political inter-
> ference by the U.S. government, which sometimes
> commands action on the part of the enterprise's
> affiliates.[5]

Diplomatic initiatives are used to resolve these home and host country policy differences.

THE NATURE OF CONTEMPORARY U.S. DIPLOMACY

No one organizational pattern for the conduct of U.S. foreign policy will ever be adopted. Each president rearranges and adjusts bureaucratic policy-making units to achieve optimal responses from overlapping, competing, and frequently conflicting institutions. As indicated in the Report on the Commission for the Reorganization of the Government in the Conduct of Foreign Policy (the Murphy Commission Report), conducting international economic policy requires the integration of foreign and domestic objectives.

Two specific organizational proposals were included in the commission's report. As indicated by Figures 2 and 3,

The responsibilities of the under secretary for economic affairs would be broadened to make this official the under secretary for economic and scientific affairs.

Responsibilities at the functional bureau level, currently divided between the Bureau of Economic and Business Affairs and the Bureau of Oceans and International Environmental and Scientific Affairs, would be expanded to form four bureaus:
- Economic and Business Affairs.
- Food, Population, and Development Affairs.
- Oceans, Environment, and Scientific Affairs.
- Transportation, Communication, and Energy Affairs. [6]

The Murphy Commission's recommendations for international economic policy matters imply an awareness of significant historical events.

Columbia University's Professor Zbigniew Brzezinski conceptualizes the importance of historical change for the United States. Brzezinski feels that a major historical post-World War II development

involves the transformation of the resource-autarkic American economy into an increasingly resource-dependent economy. Some experts have estimated that the United States is already dependent on imports for 26 out of some 36 basic raw materials consumed by its industrial economy; and this dependence is growing most dramatically, but by no means exclusively, in the energy field. This shift is imposing a mounting fiscal drain on the U.S. economy (with mineral imports costing eight billion dollars in 1970 and likely to cost about 31 billion dollars by 1985) and it also heightens the U.S. stake in a stable and uninterrupted flow of international trade. As a consequence, America finds herself so deeply involved in the world economy, a condition reinforced by its special monetary role, that on the economic plane the concept of isolationism becomes at worst a suicidal policy and at best an irrelevance.

FIGURE 2

Department of State as Currently Organized

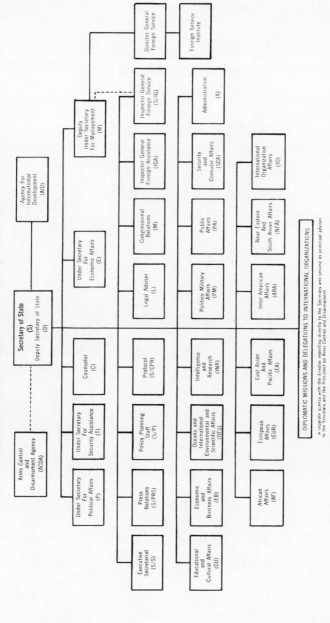

DIPLOMATIC MISSIONS AND DELEGATIONS TO INTERNATIONAL ORGANIZATIONS

A separate agency with the director reporting directly to the Secretary and serving as principal adviser to the Secretary and the President on Arms Control and Disarmament.

Source: The Murphy Commission Report, Washington, D. C. : Government Printing Office, June 27, 1975, p. 50.

FIGURE 3

Department of State as Proposed

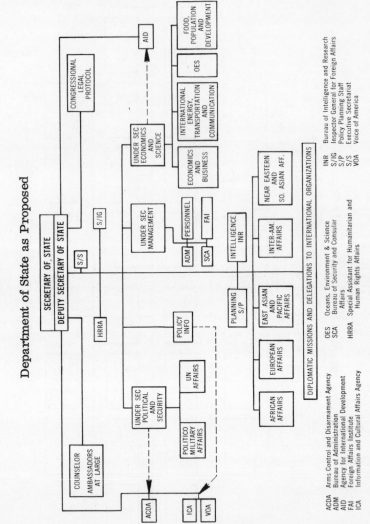

DIPLOMATIC MISSIONS AND DELEGATIONS TO INTERNATIONAL ORGANIZATIONS

ACDA	Arms Control and Disarmament Agency	OES	Oceans, Environment & Science	INR	Bureau of Intelligence and Research
ADM	Bureau of Administration	SCA	Bureau of Security and Consular	S/IG	Inspector General for Foreign Affairs
AID	Agency for International Development		Affairs	S/P	Policy Planning Staff
FAI	Foreign Affairs Institute	HRRA	Special Assistant for Humanitarian and	S/S	Executive Secretariat
ICA	Information and Cultural Affairs Agency		Human Rights Affairs	VOA	Voice of America

Source: The Murphy Commission Report, Washington, D. C. : Government Printing Office, June 27, 1975, p. 51.

66

America's growing economic interdependence with the world economy is reinforced by social dynamics, involving massive growth in tourism, in the number of Americans studying abroad and of foreigners here, in communications in general—in all of which the United States is the pacesetter. This process creates further links, transforming America's relationship with the world from one which in the past could enjoy the alternatives of isolationism or internationalism into one in which only the forms and degrees of interdependence are the issue.[7]

A contrasting view is held by academics like Harvard Professor Samuel P. Huntington. In Huntington's research, he finds that some observers

have seen the rise of the transnational organization, particularly the "multinational" business corporation, as challenging the future of the nation-state. As one leading American banker put it, "the political boundaries of nation-states are too narrow and constricted to define the scope and sweep of modern business." We have, consequently, seen the rise of "the new globalists," the "advance men" of "economic one-worldism" who see "the entire world as a market," and we may be evolving into a period in which "businessmen often wear the robes of diplomats" and "are more influential than statesmen in many quarters of the globe."[8]

Huntington remains skeptical of this assertion.

The nature of contemporary U.S. diplomacy centers upon reconciling the diverse views of policy analysts like Brzezinski and Huntington. While no one policy analyst can offer definitive advice to U.S. MNBs interested in East-West trade and investment issues, Huntington's remarks on the relationship between national governments and global enterprises should be understood. Huntington believes:

The conflict between national governments and transnational organizations is clearly complementary rather than duplicative. It is conflict not between likes but between unlikes, each of which has its own primary set of functions to perform. It is, consequently, conflict which, like labor-management conflict, involves

the structuring of relations and the distribution of benefits
to entities which need each other even as they conflict
with each other. The balance of influence may shift
back and forth from one to the other but neither can
displace the other. [9]

One's acceptance of this view leads to a consideration of U.S. MNBs
as political actors.

THE U.S. MNB AS POLITICAL ACTOR

In a speech before the Economic Club of Detroit on
February 18, 1975, Deputy Secretary of State Robert S. Ingersoll
outlined the importance of U.S. trade. It is an issue in which U.S.
MNBs have an indispensable role to play. In part, Ingersoll said,

Economics and politics have become inseparable ingredients
of international affairs. Any breakdown in the world
economic order would have political consequences—at home
and abroad—and deep concern to all of us. The State
Department is determined to improve its ability to deal
with the global economy but we do not pretend to be a
monopoly on economic wisdom. The Administration and
this Secretary of State are acutely aware of the require-
ment to read the business community into the foreign
policy process. I encourage you to join us in the search
for improved means to get our ideas across and talk out
our problems. [10]

In essence, U.S. government officials like Ingersoll see a
definite role for U.S. MNBs in the conduct of the United States'
foreign commercial relations.

Other observers support Deputy Secretary Ingersoll's position.
For example, Richard Eells believes the evolving nature of nation-
state sovereignty has permitted U.S. MNBs to achieve legitimate
status as corporate actors in the international political system.
Eells reasons,

The modern state is not the only institution established
by men to reach their objectives, and in the world arena
it becomes more and more obvious that the sovereign
state sometimes stands dangerously in the way of new
and needed institutions. We cling to the idea of the
state and of national independence because it is an

anchor to windward in a tumultuous age of rapid social
change and stupendous confrontations of power. The
nation-state does serve purposes that cannot be served
in any other way, not least in carving out parts of the
earth's surface where reliable jurisdiction makes the
framework for a life of meaning and human dignity.

When all this has been conceded, however, we
face the fact that there are and must be new dimensions
of international law to make room for intermediate institutions: instruments for getting things done in the
world arena that must be done and cannot be done by
states or public international organizations alone.
Here enters the case for recognition of private
international organizations, private corporations, and
individuals as participants and subjects of international
law. [11]

In short, Eells insists that U.S. MNBs have become international
political actors because of the expanding global sovereignty the
United States exercises as a superindustrialized nation-state. Yet
other academics, such as Jack N. Behrman, would trace the origin
of U.S. multinational businessmen's international political
activities to the emerging partnership of the government of the
United States with its multinational enterprises.

Behrman finds that the functions of governments affect
business in three ways:

(1) Business activities overseas help create the
environment in which governmental policies are
made or induce problems which alter policies of
the government, (2) governmental policies set the
stage for business operations and frequently
reverse them or alter profit expectations and (3)
there is need for more coordination of business
and governmental objectives, policies and
operations. [12]

Unfortunately, the U.S. government remains heir to a lack of
cooperation between business and government.

Behrman's expertise allows him to place the activities of
U.S. MNBs as political actors in proper perspective. He notes,

Little concerted effort is being directed toward the
long-run techniques of government-business cooperation.
This is partly a result of a lack of knowledge on the

part of business and government as to what can or
should be done, partly a result of lack of clear
understanding as to the mutuality or conflict of
interest, and partly a consequence of the fact that each
continues to mistrust the motives or objectives of
the other, which is itself a function of lack of
knowledge. Both government officials and businessmen
need to recognize their interdependence and place a
higher priority on working together in mutual trust.
For U.S. international business this may be a long road,
but we need to select the road and begin the journey. [13]

Past efforts in these areas have usually involved U.S. government
task forces and business advisory groups. Task forces are
created to bring forth new and daring ideas and to achieve a
compromise between opposing groups.

The 1973 Trade Act, Public Law 93-618, provides the most
recent example of business advisory groups. To provide overall
advice on U.S. multilateral trade objectives, President Ford
appointed a Policy Advisory Committee for Trade Negotiations.
In addition to the Policy Advisory Committee for Trade Negotiations,
the 1973 Trade Act also established private sector advisory
committees for industry, agriculture, and labor. Clearly,

these programs aim to insure that representatives of
industry, agriculture and labor can transmit views directly to
U.S. negotiators. Because of their special knowledge of U.S.
and foreign market conditions, these representatives can provide
U.S. negotiators with valuable assistance and informed judgments
regarding negotiating objectives, with emphasis on identifying
opportunities for expanding U.S. exports. The advisory committees
established as part of each consultative program will be charged
with conducting detailed studies by product sectors to determine U.S.
negotiating objectives at the product level. [14]

U.S. MNBs have been encouraged to become political
actors but in decidedly advisory roles. Under a joint Commerce-
Special Trade Representative for Trade Negotiations program,
public meetings attended by over 600 U.S. industry representatives
resulted in an Industry Consultations Program. This program
consists of a single high-level Industry Policy Advisory Committee
(IPAC) and 26 Industry Sector Advisory Committees (ISACs) covering
the entire range of U.S. industrial production. [15] The IPAC and
ISACs symbolize an institutionalization of the role of U.S. MNBs
in the conduct of U.S. multilateral trade negotiations.

On the one hand, IPAC represents a cross section of the
industrial community. It

> has the responsibility for providing policy advice
> to the Administration on the interests of industry
> as a whole. This committee will review the
> overall ISAC work program, keep informed as to
> the nature and progress of that work, and review
> the output of the 26 sector committees in terms of
> consistency with overall industry interest. Con-
> sequently, each member of the IPAC has assumed
> a liaison role with one or more of the ISAC. [16]

Organized by product sectors or subsectors, the ISACs furnish
specific advice on U.S. and foreign trade barriers affecting
individual products. The Department of Commerce prepares the
initial draft advisory report of the ISACs.

The important contribution of U.S. MNBs serving on ISACs
cannot be overlooked. Clearly,

> once formal negotiations begin the functions of the advisory
> committees will change. As events dictate, the advice
> given to U.S. negotiators in the initial ISAC reports
> may need to be revised to reflect changing conditions,
> as those reports are intended to be up-to-date functional
> documents. The committees also will be convened from
> time to time to advise on specific issues which arise
> during the negotiations. For example, to the extent
> that the value or validity of various offers, counter
> offers, and packages of concessions is not clear or
> available in the initial ISAC reports, the negotiators
> will want and need additional industry advice as those
> specific situations arise. To facilitate this continuing
> consultative process, liaison between Commerce/STR
> and the advisory committee members will be maintained
> throughout the negotiations.
>   A large part of the continuing role of the advisory
> committees was stipulated by Congress in the Trade Act,
> which requires that as agreements are concluded for
> each sector, the committee must report their views on
> those agreements to the President, Congress, and the
> STR. Those views are to encompass the extent of
> the economic impact of such agreements on the United
> States and whether sectors agreements are equitable and
> within the sector. Finally, the Industry Policy Advisory

Committee and 26 Industry Sector Advisory Committees will submit reports at the end of the negotiations covering the trade agreements made under the Act as a whole. [17]

Thus, a direct policy input for U.S. MNBs in this particular issue-area has begun. However, in the field of East-West trade and investment, two additional issue-areas suggest U.S. MNBs may be perceived as political actors.

Intelligence Gathering and Dissemination

Frequently, U.S. MNBs are quoted as saying, "Our corporation does not make foreign policy." Although this is a technically sound statement, it should not leave the impression that, aside from supplying information, U.S. MNBs do not have a significant effect on the formulation and implementation of U.S. foreign policy. In the area of gathering and disseminating information, the MNB's input is far reaching. Clearly,

> the gathering of intelligence on conditions and situations overseas is a function of both government and business. While the government helps business in many ways through gathering and disseminating intelligence on economic, commercial, financial and political matters, there is an important potential return to the government of intelligence gathered by the business community. International business has many contacts with both industrial and governmental officials overseas which give it insights not obtained through U.S. official channels. These insights relate not only to industrial activity but also to pending legislation, policy problems, and political development. [18]

Intelligence gathered from U.S. multinational executives travelling abroad provides a critical feedback for U.S. foreign economic and commercial policies. Unhappily, U.S. MNBs may be mistakenly perceived in host countries as official agents of the U.S. intelligence community.

There is some justifiable concern by foreign businessmen that links between U.S. MNBs and the Central Intelligence Agency (CIA) may exist. In the past in terms of supporting private business firms, cases exist where the CIA has operated its own commercial proprietary organizations. One such organization is Air America.

According to Victor Marchetti and John D. Marks, former CIA officials,

> Before the ceasefire in Vietnam, Air America was
> flying 125 planes of its own, with roughly 40 more
> on lease, and it had about 5000 employees, roughly
> 10 percent of whom were pilots. It was one of
> America's largest airlines, ranking just behind
> National in total number of planes. [19]

The size of Air America's operation caused U.S. domestic airlines to compete with this CIA organization. Without doubt, the CIA's interface with U.S. MNCs and MNBs must be clarified. If U.S. MNBs are inappropriately associated with clandestine activities, their ability to provide commercial information and cultivate legitimate overseas business opportunities will be severely limited. As political actors; U.S. MNB's input into U.S. foreign policy would then cease.

Securing Industrial Property Rights

When they demand industrial property rights, U.S. MNBs may be considered political actors by host country officials. Basically,

> The rights protected are patents, trademarks, and
> know-how. The first two have to be registered with
> each national government in order to receive protection
> in the market; know-how is protected in the courts only.
> These rights are the basis not only for the protection of
> exported items but also for the licensing of the right
> to manufacture by a protected process. They also
> become the basis for contributions from partners to
> a joint venture, usually being exchanges for equity.
> Since international business depends heavily on
> product differentiation and quality, business relies
> heavily on protection of differences.
> The U.S. government, for its part, is interested
> in such protection as a means of increasing U.S. sales
> abroad, of gaining royalties brought back to the United
> States to alleviate pressures on the U.S. balance of pay-
> ments, and of maintaining a technological lead in key
> industries. It has therefore become increasingly in-
> terested in international accords covering industrial
> property, particularly, patents. [20]

Although U. S. MNBs may assume that these rights are universally guaranteed, Eastern European governments perceive the insistence upon those rights as U. S. MNBs undermining the control of their socialist, nonmarket societies. It is especially critical that U. S. MNBs understand this perspective, particularly from the Soviet viewpoint, if long-term Soviet-American commercial ties are to be strengthened.

Executive-Diplomat Consultations

Questions on intelligence gathering and securing industrial property rights lead Eastern bloc countries to perceive U. S. MNBs as political actors. In practice, U. S. MNBs have previously encountered obstacles to influencing U. S. government foreign policy. The fundamental question remains: How does a U. S. MNB become a political actor? A simple answer can be found in executive-diplomat consultations. Clearly, there is

> a premium on businessmen who have served in government and can understand not only the policy purposes but also the bureaucratic methods of government. This under-standing need not cause them to "sell out" legitimate business interests; rather it should cause them not to insist on policies or procedures which are unacceptable to the government. [21]

Yet even former government officials find a variety of procedural inadequacies inhibit U. S. MNBs from becoming political actors and engaging in mutually beneficial executive-diplomat consultations. For U. S. multinational executives to play an optimal role in the conduct of U. S. foreign policy on East-West trade and investment questions, the lead and lag time between the government's consultation with U. S. MNBs must be adjusted.

Although the U. S. government seeks to promote cooperative relationships between diplomats and businessmen, a tension will always exist between them. By examining the attributes of diplomats and those of U. S. MNBs, it is possible to understand more fully the contributions each makes to U. S. foreign economic policy. If East-West economic detente is to proceed, it must be implemented by a close working partnership between U. S. multinational executives and diplomatic officials.

ATTRIBUTES OF U.S. DIPLOMATS

The leading spokesman of today's U.S. diplomats is Secretary of State Kissinger. He has aptly categorized the role behavior of diplomats and statesmen, finding,

> Statesmen must act, even when premises cannot be proved; they must decide, even when intangibles will determine the outcome. Yet predictions are impossible to prove; consequences avoided are never evident. Skepticism and suspicion thus become a way of life. [22]

Diplomats' professional characteristics are not subject to precise generalizations.

Often weak generalizations about U.S. diplomats treat them as homogeneous members of a monolithic foreign service elite. For example, it has been said,

> If foreign policy decision-makers are recruited predominantly from the business community, their convictions are more likely to coincide with those of business than with other segments of society. Recruitment creates a climate of opinion in policymaking circles which is likely to recognize the legitimacy of business interests before those of other segments of society. Businessmen in public service are likely to perceive the national interest in terms of business interests. [23]

However, no truly adequate method exists to verify such generalizations. Images and perceptions of U.S. diplomats are derived from their career orientation. Indeed, the source of a foreign policy decision maker's influence emerges from his career pattern. The career pattern molds a diplomat's bureaucratic loyalties, background, political socialization, and operational effectiveness.

Numerous studies examine the characteristics, norms, and attitudes of U.S. diplomats as members of a professional group. John Harr found that a wide range of factors determine the successful Foreign Service Officer (FSO). The most critical factor was the diplomat's ability to win the respect of his colleagues in the FSO Corps.

Dr. David Garnham, a political scientist at the University of Wisconsin has also researched the attributes of U.S. diplomats. Garnham finds,

There is a broad consensus that the State Department is
one of the more inept institutions of the U.S. government.
Because State's performance is considered mediocre,
and because the Foreign Service officer corps is the
Department's most important personnel group, (although
only twelve percent of State's employees are FSOs), it
is not surprising that the Foreign Service is often blamed
for State's difficulties. A chronic criticism is that
State's officials are timid, rigid, and noncreative.
Nearly everyone who is exposed to the Department
receives an impression of pervasive conservatism. [24]

To test the quality of State Department rigidity, Garnham offers
a psychological hypothesis which asserts,

State is rigid because the Department's employees, and
especially Foreign Service officers, are inflexible.
We know that some individuals are more rigid and
cautious than others, and we would expect an organization
to resist change if the average rigidity of its personnel
was high. [25]

Garnham's empirical evidence does not support the psychological
hypothesis. In concluding his study, he noted that,

Foreign Service psychological flexibility is
homogeneous and high. . . . One plausible alternative to the psychological explanation of State
Department conformity is a "systemic" hypothesis
which is based on the fact that human behavior is
strongly influenced by social context. This hypothesis
emphasizes characteristics of the State Department
social system. The systemic hypothesis assumes
that FSOs are not more rigid than other individuals
of similar age, education, and intelligence; it suggests,
rather, that professional diplomats work within a
social milieu which induces conformist behavior. The
promotion process is a part of the Department's social
system which can serve as an example. [26]

Thus, having failed to confirm the psychological explanation of
State Department rigidity, Garnham feels the systemic hypothesis
is a plausible alternative:

The central assumption of the systemic hypothesis is
that even highly flexible individuals will behave cautiously
if they perceive that caution is rewarded and innovation
is penalized. [27]

In another study, Garnham has examined the charge of foreign
service elitism. Garnham's findings demonstrate that

Actually, there is no statistically significant
relationship between several personal background characteristics of Foreign Service officers and FSO career
satisfaction, international-mindedness, or psychological
flexibility. It appears unlikely that Foreign Service
elitism has any impact upon the conduct of U.S. foreign
affairs. [28]

As the aforementioned studies indicate, U.S. MNBs may be
mistaken if they perceive U.S. diplomats as possessing attributes
of professional inflexibility or personal rigidity. These qualities
do not hamper U.S. diplomats in receiving input from U.S. MNBs
on U.S. foreign policy in the East-West trade and investment areas.
Although the State Department as an institution may cause its
spokesmen to respond cautiously to U.S. MNB's initiatives on such
policy questions, executive-diplomat cooperation can prove mutually
rewarding. In the field of U.S. foreign policy, the input U.S. MNBs
can make is derived from their personal attributes.

ATTRIBUTES OF U.S. MNBs

Peter F. Drucker, the respected international management
consultant and author, defines executives as

those knowledge workers, managers, or individual
professionals who are expected by virtue of their position
or their knowledge to make decisions in the normal
course of their work that have significant impact on
the performance and results of the whole. [29]

As executives, U.S. MNBs share in the planning, organizing, and
integrating of their corporations' objectives. Each executive
concentrates on selected objectives in major areas, such as production, finance, marketing or the like, which produce optimal
benefits to his MNC. Like diplomats, U.S. MNBs exude versatile
talents.

There are three wide-ranging tasks for U.S. MNBs. According to Peter Drucker,

> The first is to make economic resources economically productive. The manager has an entrepreneurial job, a job of moving resources from yesterday into tomorrow; a job not of minimizing risk, but of maximizing opportunity. . . .
> Then there is a managerial or "administrative" job of making human resources productive, of making people work together, bringing to a common task their individual skills and knowledge; a job of making strengths productive and weaknesses irrelevant, which is the purpose of organization.
> Then there is a third function. Whether they like it or not, managers are not private, in the sense that what they do does not matter. They are public. They are visible. They represent. They stand for something in the community. In fact, they are the only leading group in society--not just the business manager, but all the executives of organizations in this developed, highly organized, highly institutionalized society. Managers have a public function. [30]

To understand the interplay of the entrepreneurial, managerial and public tasks of U.S. MNBs, it is necessary to examine the attributes of multinational executives.

Thomas Aitken has categorized the attributes of U.S. MNBs. He feels the manager abroad must (a) be adept at dealing with abstractions and variables, (b) have a flair for conceptual synthesis, (c) have a high degree of sensitivity, and (d) have a firm sense of values. [31]

All MNBs are accountable for attainment of the profit goals and objectives set by their MNCs. This is especially true for the U.S. MNB operating abroad. He functions as a strategist and planner because:

1. A greater proportion of his energies is focused on new ventures and new products.

2. There is a geographical and time distance between him and his home office.

3. He is operating outside the established organization, although within its directives.

4.   Inevitably, because of a different environment, his management processes must be different, despite all efforts to make them cohere with the parent company's philosophy. [32]

In short, U.S. MNBs are human operating resources, informants, and policy makers.

As human operating resources, U.S. multinational executives take charge of general and specialized functions. Some specialized activities and duties include:

1.   Appraisal of company products, know-how, and other assets with a view to their export or commercial exploitation in areas outside the United States

2.   Evaluation of the potentials of various overseas markets and determination of priorities in timing and methods of developing them

3.   Development and administration of the export marketing of products manufactured in the United States

4.   Exploration and evaluation of opportunities for licensing and/or contract manufacturing in overseas markets

5.   Recommendation and implementation of acquisitions and/or equity investments in new manufacturing and sales facilities overseas

6.   Direction and/or coordination of the manufacturing, marketing, and service operations of foreign subsidiaries and affiliates

7.   Recommendations on appropriations for new investment, sources and uses of funds, dividend and reinvestment decisions, and other financial matters

8.   Representation and advancement of company interests in dealings and negotiations with foreign governments and private organizations, and the maintenance of favorable liaison and working relationships with them

9.   Serving on the board of directors of foreign subsidiaries and affiliated companies overseas. [33]

Given these wide-ranging functions, the decision process for U.S. MNBs clearly differs from that of U.S. government officials.

Just as the State Department, as a systemic or institutional influence, affects the kinds of decisions and role behavior of U.S. diplomats, U.S. MNCs affect the role behavior of their business spokesmen. MNCs like Exxon, General Motors, or IBM are associated with a global management approach. In other words,

1. A world corporation typically has multiple producing and marketing units located in a number of different countries, and is deriving a substantial and growing share of its total earnings from export and overseas operations. (While size and geographic spread of operations are not enough in themselves to qualify a company as a world corporation, companies rarely develop a global point of view and global management policies until they have a substantial financial stake in foreign markets.)

2. Its management recognizes the United States as part of a single world market, and the United States company as involved in international competition in its domestic operations as well as overseas.

3. United States operations are managed as one part of a total world-wide enterprise, with all investment and business opportunities weighted in the light of alternatives available elsewhere in the world.

4. Over-all company profits, rather than the sales or profit achievements of individual operating units, are the guiding consideration in management planning, and in the evaluation of management performance.

5. Responsibility for strategic planning, coordination, and control of world-wide operations is vested in top corporate officials and centralized at corporate headquarters (which will probably be in the United States but could be elsewhere).

6. Responsibility for production, marketing, and other line operations is decentralized to encourage optimum planning, profit responsibilities, and freedom of action at the local, national, and regional levels in achieving approved corporate goals. [34]

In terms of global management, the elements of an American multinational businessman's decision process includes:

1. The clear realization that the problem was generic and could be solved only through a decision that established a rule, a principle

2. The definition of the specifications which the answer to the problem had to satisfy, that is, of the "boundary conditions"

3. The thinking through what is "right," that is, the solution that will fully satisfy the specifications before attention is given to the compromises, adaptations, and concessions needed to make the decision acceptable

4. The building into the decision of the action to carry it out

5. The "feedback" which tests the validity and effectiveness of the decision against the actual course of events. [35]

Thus, allowing for decision-making lead and lag times, differing definitions of the problems and informational uncertainty, U. S. MNB's decision-making operations do not involve the crisis management nature of political, diplomatic decisions.

Those who have successfully moved from business into government service have the clearest understanding of the differences in operating styles between U. S. MNBs and government officials. Frederic V. Malek, a former Deputy Undersecretary of Health, Education and Welfare, and a special assistant to President Nixon, has itemized some of these differences. His list includes:

1. Ability to communicate
2. Sensitivity and empathy
3. Mental toughness
4. Flexibility and humility. [36]

While Malek may be proposing a set of ideal attributes for U. S. MNBs, it is usually thought that

> The most general of the reasons for the failure of success-
> ful businessmen in government is a lack of breadth—an
> inability to conceptualize rather than merely achieve, an
> inability to understand and be effective in the relations
> elements of a government role, and an inability to
> deal with problems indirectly rather than through
> authoritarian line control. [37]

For a U. S. MNB to have an input in U. S. government foreign policy-making processes, he must accommodate himself to the special subtleties of government. In essence,

> He must be endowed with sensitivity and empathy to
> human motives and problems and have a flexibility of
> mind, a high tolerance for frustration and even abuse,
> and a good deal of humility. A sense of humor is no
> detriment either.
>
> And he must have, in today's political setting, an
> abundant charisma and ability to communicate with all
> his constituent publics—including the Congress—force-
> fully and persuasively. [38]

The closest approximation to this type of U. S. MNB is the professional generalist manager.

THE PROFESSIONAL GENERALIST MANAGER

Herbert J. Kindl, general manager, Armament Systems Department of the General Electric Company, defines professional generalist managers in terms of the capability to effect cross-functional decision making in an organization. [39] Cross-functional decision making is

> a general term used to describe a process of decision making across such functional organizations as marketing, engineering, manufacturing, etc., wherein the results offer a wider range of viable solution options than any singular functional viewpoint. [40]

According to Kindl, particular attributes characterize the professional generalist manager.

Specialized knowledge alone does not predict a professional generalist manager's success. While it is important,

> it is growth in his <u>knowledgeability</u> that must accompany an incumbent manager as he matures into a professional generalist manager. His knowledgeability, his state of being knowledgeable, must be nurtured during his role maturation from problem solver to problem finder to opportunity finder. [41]

In this latter role, as opportunity finder, the U.S. multinational businessman's input into U.S. foreign policy-making process appears likely.

Prior to his maturation as an opportunity finder, a U.S. multinational businessman who is a professional generalist manager would have experience as a problem solver and problem finder. Based upon more than 20 years of industrial management experience, Kindl finds,

> performing as a problem solver, the lower functional manager relies on <u>methods</u> or techniques knowledge derived from an organization's operations, reports, manuals, etc. As a problem finder, the maturing manager develops his repetoire of <u>realities</u> knowledge. Such knowledge may be less useful for immediate problem solving, but more valuable in gaining understanding of problem origins, trends, relations and impact on his business. This knowledge is equally important to him for problem prognosis and diagnosis. [42]

However,

> As an opportunity finder, the matured professional
> generalist manager develops goals knowledge to
> formulate his business' philosophy, policy and
> objectives. It is this role of exploiting opportunities
> that his decision making comprises a three-fold process
> of defining the configuration of response he desires
> from subordinates; effecting participative management
> with them; and assessing performance against the
> configuration of response desired. He creates the
> options for his responsible team members to
> consider by managing ideas rather than people. [43]

Kindl's formulation applies to the U.S. MNB's input in the conduct of
U.S. government East-West trade and investment policies.
Specifically,

> cross-functional decision making begins with the process
> of defining the configuration of response desired that will
> resolve a particular problem or opportunity. Preparing
> a configuration of response is an act, by one ultimately
> responsible for problem results, that provides the
> general framework in which subsequent decisions are
> made. It defines the response approach to be pursued
> by subordinates. The intent is to put into perspective
> the desired result with its associated, acceptable
> levels of risk. It sets the constraints of cost,
> schedule and technical performance against which
> acceptable solutions are offered to resolve problems
> and opportunities. [44]

In short, U.S. MNBs should present to U.S. government officials
responsible for East-West trade and investment policies a clear
picture as to what policies are desirous for their multinational
corporation's needs or international business opportunities.

By defining their assumptions and alternatives together with
the levels of political risk associated with East-West trade and
investment policies, U.S. MNBs could involve U.S. government
officials in cooperative policy partnerships. Commercial, economic
policy evolved from executive-diplomat partnerships should be
more balanced than policy formulated entirely by U.S. government
officials. However, before U.S. government officials accept a direct
policy input from U.S. MNBs, multinational executives must
demonstrate a willingness to participate openly in the politics of the
executive branch bureaucracy.

U. S. MNBs' ROLE IN EAST-WEST POLITICS

As previously described, U. S. diplomats and MNBs possess distinct attributes. When added to institutional ties, these personal qualities indicate the kind of inputs expected from each on issues of East-West trade and investment. Indeed, U. S. diplomats and MNBs may have alternative belief systems. Frequently, the existence of separate belief systems or institutional commitments prevent U. S. MNBs from actively participating in the formulation process and conduct of U. S. international economic policy. Traditionally,

the businessman's role in politics is an old question which resurfaces unfailingly each election year. Both those who favor and those who disfavor executive political involvement give many compelling reasons. The real dilemma, however, belongs to those within the corporation who determine policy: what course should the corporation take either to elicit or prohibit political participation in its executives. [45]

The past literature on this subject shows that a wide variety of these variables, which are particularly important in explaining the corporate impact upon the political behavior of executives, has been suggested:

1. The existence or absence of special, politically oriented functions such as legal or public relations departments.
2. Company policy regarding political activity.
3. Company incentives for alternate activities to politics, the potential rewards of these alternatives, and the ease with which they may be undertaken.
4. Executive self-restraint based upon negative views of politicians and upon perceptions of business-government and executive-politician interactions.
5. External controls such as legal constraints. The many available variables which influence executive political activity have yet to be assembled in any organized and meaningful fashion. [46]

Accepting this problem, in our area of concern, if U. S. MNBs are to become more politically active, they must understand the nature of East-West trade and investment policies. Therefore, before comparing how U. S. multinational businessmen's and government officials' views differ on the roles open to multinational executives in foreign economic policy participation, a few critical East-West trade and investment policy issues will be examined.

NOTES

1. Chadwick F. Alger, "The Multinational Corporation and the Future International System," in The Multinational Corporation, ed. David H. Blake (The Annals of the American Academy of Political and Social Science, Vol. 403, September 1972), pp. 105-06.

2. Jacques G. Maisonrouge, "How a Multinational Corporation Appears to Its Managers," in Global Companies: The Political Economy of World Business, ed. George W. Ball (Englewood Cliffs, N. J.: Prentice-Hall, Inc., 1975), p. 15.

3. Ibid., p. 19.

4. See Richard J. Barnet and Ronald E. Muller, Global Reach: The Power of the Multinational Corporations (New York: Simon and Schuster, 1975), pp. 1-389, and Raymond Vernon, Sovereignty at Bay: The Multinational Spread of U.S. Enterprises (New York: Basic Books, Inc., 1971), pp. 1-284.

5. Jack N. Behrman, National Interests and the Multinational Enterprise, Tensions Among the North Atlantic Countries (Englewood Cliffs, N. J.: Prentice-Hall, Inc., 1970), p. 8.

6. Robert D. Murphy, Chairman, Commission on the Organization of the Government for the Conduct of Foreign Policy, report, Washington, D. C.: Government Printing Office, June 27, 1975, p. 49, hereafter cited as The Murphy Commission Report.

7. Zbigniew Brzezinski, "U.S. Foreign Policy: The Search for Focus," Foreign Affairs 51, no. 4 (July 1973): 710-11.

8. Samuel P. Huntington, "Transnational Organizations in World Politics," World Politics 25, no. 3 (April 1973): 363.

9. Ibid., p. 366.

10. Robert S. Ingersoll, "The Global Economy," address by the deputy secretary of state before the Economic Club of Detroit, Cobo Hall, Detroit, Michigan, February 18, 1975, Washington, D. C.: Department of State Press Release no. 74, p. 8.

11. Richard Eells, Global Operations: The Emerging System of World Economic Power (New York: Interbook, Inc., 1972), pp. 80-81.

12. Jack N. Behrman, U.S. International Business and Governments (New York: McGraw-Hill, 1971), p. 12.

13. Ibid., p. 13.

14. "Businessmen to Play Key Role in Advising U.S. Negotiators at Coming World Trade Talks," Commerce Today 5, no. 7 (January 6, 1975): 20, hereafter cited as "Businessmen's Role in World Trade Talks."

15. "Businessmen's Role in World Trade Talks," p. 20.

16. Ibid.

17. Ibid. , p. 20-21.

18. Behrman, op cit, p. 154-55.

19. Victor Marchetti and John D. Marks, The CIA and the Cult of Intelligence (New York: Alfred A. Knopf, Inc. , 1974), p. 153.

20. Behrman, pp. 164-65.

21. Ibid. , p. 242.

22. Henry A. Kissinger, "U.S. Foreign Policy: Finding Strength Through Adversity," Address before the American Society of Newspaper Editors, April 17, 1975, Washington, D. C. : Department of State, Office of Media Services, press release no. 204, p. 3.

23. Dennis M. Ray, "Corporations and American Foreign Relations," in The Multinational Corporation, ed. David H. Blake (The Annals of the American Academy of Political and Social Science, Vol. 403, September 1972), pp. 89-90.

24. David Garnham, "State Department Rigidity: Testing a Psychological Hypothesis, " International Studies Quarterly, 18, no. 1 (March 1974): 31.

25. Ibid. , p. 32.

26. Ibid. , pp. 37-38.

27. Ibid. , p. 38.

28. David Garnham, "Foreign Service Elitism and U. S. Foreign Affairs," Public Administration Review 35, no. 1 (January- February 1975): 44.

29. Peter F. Drucker, The Effective Executive (New York: Harper & Row, 1967), p. 8.

30. Peter Drucker, Technology, Management and Society (New York: Harper & Row, 1970), pp. 93, 96.

31. Thomas Aitken, The Multinational Man: The Role of the Manager Abroad (New York: John Wiley and Sons, 1973), p. 15.

32. Ibid. , p. 45.

33. Enid Baird Lovell, The Changing Role of the International Executive (New York: National Industrial Conference Board, Inc. , Business Policy Study no. 119, 1966), p. 57.

34. Ibid. , p. 152.

35. Drucker, The Effective Executive, pp. 122-23.

36. Frederic V. Malek, "Mr. Executive Goes to Washington," Harvard Business Review 50, no. 5 (September-October 1972): 67-68.

37. Ibid. , p. 68.

38. Ibid.

39. Herbert J. Kindl, "The Professional Generalist Manager," Defense Management Journal 11, no. 1 (January 1975): 55.

40. Ibid. , p. 55.

41. Ibid.

42. Ibid. , p. 56.

43. Ibid. , p. 56.

44. Ibid.

45. Powell and Hostiuck, "The Business Executive's Role in Politics," Business Horizons 15, no. 4 (August 1972): 49.

46. Ibid. , p. 50.

5

EAST-WEST TRADE
AND INVESTMENT ISSUES

The Arab oil embargo of the United States in the fall of 1973 indicated the United States was living in an age of scarce global resources. Charles W. Robinson, former president of the Marcona Corporation and now undersecretary of state for economic affairs, has analyzed the implications of this event. He believes, "With growing supply and demand imbalances in other basic resources, it would seem that increasing government involvement in our business planning is inevitable. Shouldn't business leaders take the initiative as architects of a new structure of business/government relations?"[1] If U. S. MNBs follow Undersecretary Robinson's advice and develop meaningful executive/diplomat relationships on East-West matters, they must understand the complex issues and policies facing U. S. government officials. In this chapter, three issues are analyzed. The issues depict the kinds of problems drawing U. S. MNBs and U. S. policy makers toward formulating cooperative solutions. In relying on one another, U. S. MNBs and U. S. policy makers share mutual benefits. The benefits derive from a two-way exchange of information and expertise. This two-way flow recognizes the need for the U. S. MNB to have a clearly designated role in the conduct of U. S. international economic policy.

COMMODITY TRADING WITH THE SOVIET UNION
AND THE EASTERN BLOC COUNTRIES

Harold Geneen, chairman and chief executive of ITT, believes, "America, by bringing its technological and industrial strength to bear, has the opportunity to lead the world into a new age of nutrition."[2]

In an era of economic and political detente, the United States seeks
to share the benefits and burdens of global nutrition leadership with
the Soviet Union and her Eastern European trade partners. Presently,
the United States sells its surplus grain stocks to the Soviet Union.
These exports represent valuable dollar returns to U.S. producers.
However, strengthening the Soviet's capacity to feed its population has
been a controversial issue.

U.S. legislators question whether grain sales to the Soviets are
in the U.S. national interest. Previously, in 1972, Soviet leaders
upgraded Russian dietary standards by planning for increased meat
production. Faced with drought conditions, the Soviets bought 19
million tons, nearly 700 million bushels, of U.S. corn and wheat to
accomplish this objective. Buying swiftly and secretly, the Soviets
purchased U.S. surplus wheat and corn stocks at record low prices
of $1.48 a bushel for wheat and $1.05 a bushel for corn. By
August 1975 number 2 soft red wheat sold for $3.7325 a bushel and
number 2 yellow corn sold for $3.13 a bushel. [3] Private U.S. grain
companies, such as Cook Industries and Continental Grain, were
temporarily forced to suspend export grain sales to the Soviets in
September 1974.

While U.S. legislators respond to the economic concerns of
their constituents, U.S. grain trading companies and their executives
find their position misunderstood and unappreciated by the public.
U.S. MNBs from agricultural, food processing corporations find
themselves blessed and cursed simultaneously. On the one hand,
U.S. MNBs are affected by Soviet grain purchasing policy. In spite
of spreading drought in the Soviet Union during the summer of 1975,
the Soviets have stuck to their goal of expanding livestock production.
Soviet leaders continue to buy grain to maintain their high per capita
consumption of bread. On a per capita basis, the Soviet Union
consumes some 550 pounds of bread a year. This compares with
85 pounds of bread a year in the United States. Thus, U.S. producers
are applauded for servicing this vast export market.

Soviet agriculture has not provided additional grain reserves
needed for growing Soviet herds or to meet Soviet grain export
commitments. Although U.S. MNBs have long sought profitable
export markets for bulk agricultural commodities, rising domestic
food prices have placed multinational grain executives in a whirlwind
of political abuse. President Ford must weigh the balance-of-payments
advantage of large export grain sales to the Soviets against the
inflationary pressures mounting in the United States' commodity
markets. Critics of current international commodity practices often
use U.S. grain companies and their executives as convenient scape-
goats. In the chess game of economic detente with the Soviets, U.S.
MNBs can easily be blamed for causing domestic price rises but

haltingly praised for developing long-term Eastern European commodity export markets.

An examination of U. S. foreign agricultural trade statistics
indicate that a wide variety of Eastern European commodity export
markets have been developed by U. S. businessmen. The value of
U. S. agricultural exports to the USSR and the Eastern bloc countries
is increasing. [4] However, the volume of U. S. exports is leveling off.
Donald Chrisler, East European area specialist in the Department
of Agriculture's Foreign Demand and Competition Division, notes,

> The value of U. S. farm sales to Eastern Europe rose
> to $500 million in 1972/73, $750 million in 1973/74, and
> are forecast at about $700 million in the current fiscal
> year. But in terms of 1971/72 prices, these exports
> would be valued at from $350 million to $400 million in
> all three years.
>
> In volume terms, U. S. shipments of feed grain,
> cattle hides, and vegetable oil are forecast to increase;
> wheat exports will decline; and sales of all other major
> commodities should level off in 1974/75. For the first
> time since 1970/71, the value of U. S. grain exports
> will exceed the value of U. S. oilseed product exports
> to Eastern Europe. *
>
> Poland will again be, by far, the major market. †
> During July 1974–January 1975, Poland received 40
> percent of direct U. S. exports to the region.
>
> This season, the USSR will continue to be the major
> supplier of wheat to Eastern Europe. The Soviet Union
> has contracted to supply 1 million tons of wheat to
> Poland and 800,000 tons of grain, mostly wheat, to
> Czechoslovakia in 1975. In addition, the USSR probably
> will deliver 1 million tons of wheat to East Germany.
> U. S. exports of wheat to the region, which exceeded
> 1 million tons in 1973/74, are forecast to decline to less
> than half that amount in the current year. Poland is
> the main destination.
>
> U. S. exports of feed grain, however, are forecast to
> increase from 1.4 million tons last year to about 2 million
> in 1974/75. Regular customers Poland and East Germany

---

* Reproduced here as Table 5.1.
† See Table 5.2.

will again head the list, followed by occasional
buyer Romania. The major portion of the U.S. feed
grain exports to Romania is being financed under a
$31 million Commodity Credit Corporation (CCC) credit.

The rapid growth in U.S. oilmeal exports to Eastern
Europe—from 240,000 tons in 1967/68 to 970,000 in 1973/
74—is forecast to level off this year. Little change
in volume is expected but lower prices will reduce the
export value sharply. All of the countries of Eastern
Europe purchased U.S. meal this year, with Poland,
Hungary, and East Germany the leading buyers.

As with wheat, the USSR dominates the East European
cotton market. Under bilateral arrangements, North
Africa and Middle Eastern countries supply most of the
remainder and the U.S. share of the market is small.
The volume of U.S. cotton exports should be about the
same as last year but, because of lower prices, the
export value will be down. Romania, the leading
customer in the region since 1970/71, will again head the
list. Virtually all of the U.S. growth are being financed
under the CCC credit program—$20 million has been
extended to Romania and $8 million to Poland to cover
1974/75 cotton purchases.

Sales of U.S. cattle hides to Eastern Europe
reached about 3 million pieces in 1972/73 and 1973/74,
and are forecast to increase in the current year. As
with oil-meal and cotton, lower prices are driving the
export value down this year. All countries in the
region purchase U.S. cattle hides, with Romania,
Poland, and Czechoslovakia continuing as the top
customers this year. [5]

Dr. Marshall I. Goldman, professor of economics at
Wellesley College, has studied the Soviet commodity purchasing
programs. He believes,

The Soviet Union has found it convenient to use
the American farmer as a buffer reserve for its own
climatic and productive inadequacies. This means that
we in the United States have to bear the cost of storing
the grain until it is needed by the Soviet Union. Similarly, we also have to suffer the high prices set off
when the episodic Soviet purchases deplete the normal
reserves built up to satisfy our regular world and
domestic needs. [6]

TABLE 5.1

Exports of U.S. Agricultural Commodities to Eastern Europe, by Commodity,
1967/68 – 1973/74*

(Millions of U.S. Dollars)

Commodity	1967/68	1968/69	1969/70	1970/71	1971/72	1972/73	1973/74
Wheat and flour	20.8	0.8	0.6	52.7	2.5	94.3	145
Feed grains	40.9	37.9	33.7	71.6	53.6	93.7	145
Grains	61.7	38.7	34.3	124.3	56.1	188.0	290
Oilseeds	6.1	7.2	21.6	23.3	9.3	40.6	55
Vegetable oil	7.6	1.5	3.9	43.5	28.3	27.8	27.2
Oilmeal	22.9	29.0	51.1	51.5	43.1	132.1	243.4
Oilseed products	36.6	37.7	76.6	118.3	80.7	200.5	325.6
Cotton	17.8	21.3	13.0	4.8	17.4	20.7	46.8
Hides and skins	5.9	9.9	13.7	15.9	28.0	69.5	56.3
Other	15.2	11.4	13.5	15.2	21.4	18.9	38.2
Total	137.2	119.0	151.1	278.5	203.6	497.6	756.9

*Adjusted for transshipments through Canada, Netherlands, and West Germany.
Source: FAE Report No. 102 (Washington, D.C.: Government Printing Office, April 1975), p. 11.

TABLE 5.2

Exports of U.S. Agricultural Commodities to Eastern Europe, by Country,
1967/68 - 1973/74*

(Millions of U.S. Dollars)

Year	Bulgaria	Czecho-slovakia	East Germany	Hungary	Poland	Romania	Yugoslavia	Total
1967/68	3.3	10.8	24.2	5.0	52.8	.5	41.2	137.8
1968/69	1.9	8.8	20.4	6.9	55.5	3.6	21.9	119.0
1969/70	4.4	14.0	29.5	12.9	53.3	15.0	22.1	151.2
1970/71	3.6	28.7	17.3	19.2	51.7	51.1	107.0	278.6
1971/72	.7	23.7	24.6	15.5	63.4	27.3	48.6	203.8
1972/73	2.0	55.2	54.8	20.8	202.0	70.5	92.4	497.7
1973/74	2.3	63.4	67.1	30.3	319.0	110.9	163.5	756.9
1974/75								
1975/76								

*Adjusted for transshipments through Canada, Netherlands, and West Germany.

Source: FAE Report No. 102 (Washington, D.C.: Government Printing Office, April 1975), p. 11.

Goldman believes in limiting Russian grain purchases. Moreover, advance notice of Soviet purchases should be publicized. This would permit U.S. commodity prices to adjust more smoothly.

Unfortunately, Goldman's view neglects two important points. First, private U.S. companies, not the U.S. government, own the grain. The companies seek to sell it at the highest profit levels. Barring any strategic controls placed on bulk commodity export sales, U.S. government prohibition of such sales drastically reduces the profit margins for U.S. producers. Second, Goldman does not emphasize that commodity trading, especially grain trading, is a highly specialized and risky business. Many smaller U.S. grain exporters suffer large-scale financial losses when the U.S. government curtails or prohibits surplus grain exports.

David M. Schoonover, an official of the USDA's Economic Research Service believes,

> Any attempt to project USSR feed trade would seem to require extreme foolhardiness. The USSR has published relatively little historical information on feed supply and utilization, livestock product demand, and foreign trade criteria. Projection of the future is a hazardous undertaking, even when the past is well documented. [7]

Nevertheless, Soviet central planners will attempt to supply livestock product output in quantities adequate to meet demonstrated demand. According to Schoonover's calculations, found in Table 5.3, Soviet grain and wheat balances should level off during 1975–76. However, as indicated in Table 5.4, a noticeable Soviet feed gap is projected. Like present-day grain sales, by 1985–86, an estimated shortfall of 102 million metric tons of oat-equivalent feed units in the Soviet Union could again lead U.S. government policy makers and U.S. MNBs into strained relationships. Fortunately, three separate programs are under way to enable U.S. MNBs to have an input in shaping selected aspects of U.S. foreign agricultural policy. These policy programs focus on the problems of international commodity export trading with the Soviet Union and the Eastern European nations.

Grain Inspection Proposals

One legislative program in the foreign agricultural policy field focuses on U.S. grain inspection procedures. Secretary of Agriculture Earl L. Butz has proposed to Congress "a cooperative

TABLE 5.3

USSR: Grain and Wheat Balances, 1970/71, and Projections for 1975/76, 1980/81, and 1985/86*

(Million Metric Tons)

Year	Supply			Exports	Distribution						Stock Change
	Total	Production	Imports		Total	Dockage and Waste	Seed	Manufacture	Food	Feed	
Grain											
1970/71	179.6	186.8	1.3	8.4	183.3	18.7	24.8	2.8	45.3	91.7	-3.7
1975/76	209.6	214.6	—	5.0	209.6	21.5	25.9	2.8	45.0	114.4	—
1980/81	238.9	243.9	—	5.0	238.9	24.4	24.9	3.0	45.4	141.2	—
1985/86	267.9	272.9	—	5.0	267.9	27.3	24.0	3.1	45.3	168.2	—
Wheat											
1970/71	93.0	99.7	0.5	7.2	97.0	10.0	13.8	0.8	35.0	37.4	-4.0
1975/76	98.2	103.2	—	5.0	98.2	10.3	13.3	0.8	35.0	38.8	—
1980/81	105.9	110.9	—	5.0	105.9	11.1	12.2	0.8	35.4	46.4	—
1985/86	112.4	117.4	—	5.0	112.4	11.7	11.2	0.8	35.3	53.4	—

*Assuming zero imports.

Source: David M. Schoonover, "The Soviet Feed-Livestock Economy: Preliminary Findings on Performance and Trade Implications," ERS Report No. 356 (Washington, D.C.: Government Printing Office, April 1974), p. 38.

TABLE 5.4

USSR: Balance of Feed Requirements and Domestic Supplies in
Oat-Equivalent Feed Units, 1970/71, and Projections for 1975/76,
1980/81, and 1985/86
(Million Metric Tons)

	Total Feed			Concentrates		
Year	Requirements	Domestic Supplies	Balance	Requirements	Domestic Supplies*	Balance
1970/71	—	†337	—	—	108	—
1975/76	399	374	-25	136	135	-1
1980/81	476	423	-53	187	165	-22
1985/86	575	473	-102	253	196	-57

*Assumes exports of 5 million tons of wheat.
†Assumes small quantities of imports.
Source: Schoonover, ERS Report No. 356, (Washington, D. C. : Government Printing Office, April 1974), p. 39.

96

Federal-state system to tighten inspection procedures in an attempt to eliminate alleged corruption in the grain-export trade of the United States."[8] Abuses in the present grain-inspection system have led to proposals for several alternative ones. Corruption in grain handling procedures have occurred because:

Under the present system, grain is inspected and graded by inspectors licensed by the Department of Agriculture but employed by private or state agencies created by boards of trade or chambers of commerce on which grain-company and shipping interests are heavily represented.

Small staffs of Federal supervisors attempt to spot-check the work of the private and state inspectors.

The system has lent itself to questions of conflicts of interest, and allegations of bribery and improper influences on inspectors have grown out of the current investigation.

In addition, foreign buyers have complained that they have received less value than they paid for. [9]

Under these circumstances, several alternative legislative programs have been proposed.

The main grain inspection proposals include:

An all-federal inspection system.

A system with some federal inspection but continuing state-agency inspection in states where such agencies already exist, with the option for other states to create such agencies.

A similar federal-state system but one that would limit state agencies to inland points and require federal inspection at all export ports.

A system that would include state, federal, and private inspections, but with the right of federal supervisors to move in and perform original inspections when situations called for the action. Under the present system, federal agents can perform only secondary inspection, either as a supervisory function or on appeal from original certification of grades.

A continuation of the present private and state system but with tightened requirements on performance and supervision.

Still another option was offered, said to combine various features of other choices. [10]

Given the nature of these proposals, U.S. MNBs have the opportunity to appeal directly to USDA officials, trade associations, members of

Congress, and the U. S. public to determine the kind of export grain inspection program required. The expertise of U. S. marketing executives familiar with Eastern European bulk commodity trading problems provides procedural guidance to U. S. government policy makers. Export commodity trading of bulk agricultural stocks forms an important instrument for implementing U. S. foreign policy objectives. U. S. MNBs can contribute to strengthening the operational components of this instrument by criticizing and evaluating alternative federal-state grain-inspection proposals.

Market Development Programs

A second program involving executive/bureaucrat cooperation is the USDA's industry-foreign market development program for U. S. agricultural products. Administered by the Foreign Agricultural Service (FAS), this program is a long-term government/ industry effort to develop, maintain, and expand commercial foreign markets for a wide variety of U. S. agricultural products in support of domestic agricultural policies and programs. USDA funds for foreign market development are made available under the Agricultural Trade Development and Assistance Act of 1954 (Public Law 480) as amended. [11]
Under this program,

> about 40 agricultural producer associations (called
> "Market Development Cooperators") work with FAS
> on a continuing basis, while about two dozen others
> undertake short-term projects. Within the United
> States, support for the program comes from more than
> 3. 5 million individual farmers, cooperatives, and ag-
> riculturally related firms (totals include some members
> counted in more than one organization). Cooperator
> activities are carried out under agreements with FAS.
> Programs are approved where there are identified
> foreign market opportunities and clear evidence that U. S.
> producers will normally produce quantities above the
> usual domestic requirements. Finally, the proposed
> program must not duplicate other programs or conduct
> activities that private industry could be expected to
> perform alone. [12]

In reality, the Foreign Agricultural Service lacks a domestic field office network like those of the Commerce Department. Yet, as indicated in Figure 4, eight of the ten leading U. S. agricultural

FIGURE 4

Ten Leading U. S. Agricultural Exports, as
Percentage of Farm Production, 1974*

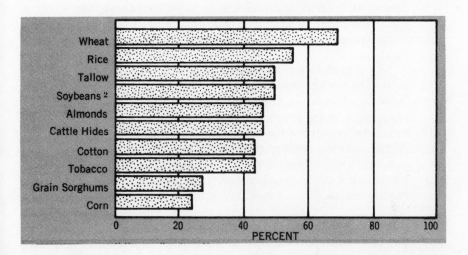

*Year ending June 30.
† Includes bean equivalent of meal.
Source: David L. Hume, "Foreign Market Development—A
Government/Industry Team," Foreign Agriculture 13, no. 21
(May 26, 1975): 4.

exports constitute more than 40 percent of the farm production of these
commodities. Darwin Stolte, chairman of the Agricultural Cooperator
Council for Market Developments, believes such large-scale bulk
commodity exports reflect the success of U. S. MNBs in joint govern-
ment-industry programs.

Describing the past 20-year history of U. S. government-
industry cooperator programs established by the 1954 Agricultural
Trade Development and Assistance Act, Stolte notes,

Cooperators are nonprofit organizations representing
producers and other sectors of agriculture in a joint
program with FAS aimed at developing foreign markets.
Each cooperator focuses on markets for products with

which its members are concerned, with the overall
result of expanding total U. S. farm trade. Today,
there are about 40 of these groups working with
GAS on a continuing basis, while another two dozen
undertake short-term projects.

The cooperators, in turn, represent a diverse and
competitive array of producers and agribusinesses. All
told, this amounts to over 3. 5 million producers, 1, 500
cooperatives, and more than 7, 000 processors and
handlers. . .

Cooperators are currently working closely with
about 130 foreign firms and trade associations. The
increasingly heavy involvement of these foreign co-
cooperators in the program reflects the mutually
beneficial results of the varied activities being conducted, and the confidence these groups have in the
U. S. agricultural production, processing, and
marketing experts working with them under the
joint program. [13]

U. S. MNBs, through FAS cooperator programs in particular commodities, have an important input in the market development activities
used to sustain U. S. foreign policy goals.

The expertise of U. S. executives forms the foundation for the
effective lobbying activities of cooperator groups like the Cotton
Council International, the Poultry and Egg Institute of America, the
American Hereford Association, the National Peanut Council, the
U. S. Tobacco Exporters Association, Inc. , and others. By expressing
their demands through these groups, U. S. MNBs can formally but
indirectly shape selected aspects of U. S. foreign agricultural policy.

U. S. /USSR Agricultural Cooperation

Executive-bureaucrat cooperation encompasses the implementation
of the U. S. -USSR Agreement on Agricultural Cooperation. This agreement, along with those in forestry, science and technology, environmental protection, and others, was signed in Washington, D. C. , on
June 19, 1973. In accordance with the Agricultural Agreement's
provisions, the Soviet Union and the United States have established
a Joint Committee on Cooperation in Agriculture. Two working
groups under the Joint Committee, the U. S. -USSR Working Group
on Agricultural Economic Research and Information and the U. S. -USSR
Working Group on Agricultural Research and Technological Development,
have been formed to cooperatively implement the agreement.

Under the Joint Committee, the United States and USSR have each established a permanent secretariat. The secretariats coordinate programs and activities formulated by the Joint Committee and its working groups. The U.S. Secretariat, located in the Foreign Agricultural Service of the USDA, administers the working group programs. In addition, the U.S. Secretariat serves as a communications link between the U.S. and USSR working groups.

Four project areas have been assigned to both working groups. For example, under the Economic Working Group, project coordinators plan and implement programs in library exchange, forecasting, economic information exchange, and agribusiness. The U.S. Research and Technology Working Group is planning and implementing plant, soil, animal science, and mechanization programs. USDA administrators from the Foreign Agricultural Service, and the Cooperative State Research Service comprise a group which provides policy and operational guidance to the U.S. Secretariat, project coordinators, working groups, and the Joint Committee. U.S. MNBs desiring an input into the implementation of the U.S.-USSR Agreement on Agricultural Cooperation can directly lobby the Administrators' Group or the U.S. Secretariat.

Together with U.S. government officials, U.S. MNBs share important responsibilities in accomplishing the primary objectives of the agricultural agreement. The exchange of information on commodity production and agricultural science research depends largely on U.S. MNBs, market development cooperator organizations, and university agricultural departments. Through the exchange of research publications, technical specialists, computer programs, and agricultural engineering instruments, U.S. MNBs can effect the qualitative results of the agreement. For whatever reason, an organized rejection of the agreement would withdraw a diplomatic tool for achieving U.S.-Soviet detente. Clearly the intensity of interest U.S. MNBs display through their contacts with the U.S. Secretariat and the Administrators' Group is important. The nature of U.S. MNBs' contacts will determine how much of a policy and/or operational role U.S. executives play in this bilateral, U.S.-USSR field of foreign agricultural policy.

EXPORT LICENSING PROBLEMS ON EASTERN EUROPEAN SALES

U.S. MNBs encounter many obstacles in establishing long-term Eastern European and Soviet sales markets. Selling industrial manufactured goods in Eastern Europe presents U.S. executives with a complex series of export licensing problems. According to Zbigniew Brzezinski, the first problem U.S. MNBs face is the cumbersome

U.S. government bureaucracy charged with administering export controls. As Figure 5 indicates, a vast array of U.S. departments and agencies are involved.

Besides coping with a multitude of U.S. government departments handling export licenses, U.S. MNBs seeking Eastern bloc and Soviet sales face extensive evaluation of their manufactured goods. The evaluation determines the strategic significance of the product and its possible alternative uses. Dr. Roger F. Shields, deputy assistant secretary of defense, notes,

> Advanced technology, in short, is a major U.S. military,
> economic and diplomatic asset. As an asset, it should
> be carefully managed. This does not imply that it
> should be indiscriminately hoarded; but it does suggest
> that when we export technology, we should assure that
> a clear and commensurate return to the United States
> will be obtained. [14]

In this area, the Department of Defense (DOD) exercises control authority in evaluating the strategic implications of proposed high-technology and capital investment projects. Moreover, DOD's security review remains unchallenged over license applications of high-technology machinery or information of potentially direct military significance.

The Defense Department's statutory authority is stated in the Export Administration Act of 1969 as amended in 1972 by the Equal Export Opportunity Act. This act authorizes controls:

> The basis for administering these controls is the
> commodity control list, which specifies items which
> may be exported only after a Government license has
> been issued by the U.S. Department of Commerce.
> This list is continuously under scrutiny and items
> are dropped or added as may be necessary to keep
> it current. [15]

For U.S. MNBs attempting to establish a sales market for high-technology products such as wide-bodied aircraft or semiconductors, the Defense Department's export license approval is critical. Frequently, an interagency operating committee must meet to evaluate a proposed sale. In general, Defense has

one senior official working full time on U.S. license applications, another on COCOM license applications, and a middle grade official who assists both of them. In addition, the director of strategic trade and

FIGURE 5

Administrative Structure of Export Controls

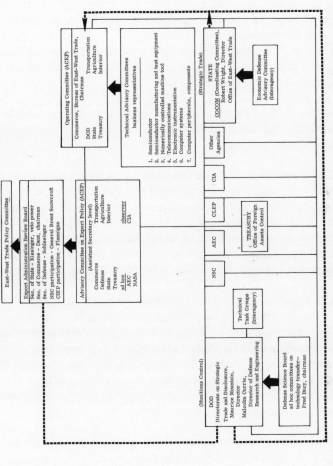

Source: U.S., Congress, Senate, Committee on Foreign Relations, Multinational Corporations and United States Foreign Policy, Hearings before the Subcommittee on Multinational Corporations, 93rd Cong., 2nd sess., on Investment by Multinational Companies in the Communist Bloc Countries, June 17, 19, and July 17, 18, 19, and 22, 1974, Part 10 (Washington, D.C.: Government Printing Office, 1975), p. 182, hereafter cited as Multinational Corporations and United States Foreign Policy, Part 10.

disclosure spends 75 percent of his time on these cases and the policy issues related to them.

While many cases can be decided by these officials on the basis of their knowledge and experience (particularly on Operating Committee cases where generally excellent analytical work has been done by commerce technical experts before they come to defense for review), a majority of the Operating Committee cases and a large number of the COCOM cases are sent to various technical and intelligence experts through the defense establishment for their review and assessment.

We are in almost daily contact with 15 or 20 specialists, and in the 3 military services alone have 18 major technical offices on which we call for support. [16]

In the area of export licenses, American MNBs need to appreciate the standard operating procedures of the Department of Defense. For example,

The number of U.S. export license requests annually reviewed by defense amounts to approximately 500 cases where a formal full-scale review takes place in the interagency Operating Committee chaired by the Department of Commerce. In addition, there are annually about 700 export cases where commerce has been granted a delegation of authority to waive Operating Committee review but must secure defense's concurrence bilaterally before issuing licenses.

The number of COCOM exception requests (exclusive of US cases) annually reviewed by defense is between 700 and 800.

A sampling of our records indicated that defense processes over 90 percent of all COCOM cases within two weeks or less of their receipt. On US cases, 85 percent of the less complex ones are dealt with by defense in less than two weeks, while of those referred to the Operating Committee approximately 90 percent are processed in defense within three weeks. [17]

While corporate executives have to adapt to Defense Department rulings, U.S. government officials must be sensitive to U.S. MNBs' concerns. Dr. C. Lester Hogan of the Fairchild Camera and Instrument Corporation explained these concerns for Senator Frank Church, Chairman of the U.S. Senate Foreign Relations Subcommittee on Multinational Corporations. Fairchild represents a medium-sized manufacturing company. Because of its high-technology products, Hogan estimated that 30 percent of Fairchild's current sales derive from products less than two years old. [18] Speaking of the semiconductor industry as a whole, Hogan stated,

Our industry faces bitter and constant price competition
from European and Japanese semiconductor firms, which
have lower production costs and various nontariff barriers
to protect their home markets from our competition. . . .

If high volume sales are crucial to the American
semiconductor industry's competitive position, then
foreign sales are becoming increasingly significant in
terms of maintaining that volume. [19]

Hogan represents a responsible U. S. multinational business
executive. Research studies he commissioned for Fairchild vividly
depict the importance of the Eastern European semiconductor
market. In part, Hogan's research indicates that

Eastern Europe is the last sizeable, commercial market
which has not been tapped by the U. S. semiconductor
industry or its Japanese or European competitors.
There is no other comparable region possessing the
potentially huge consumer demand for products utilizing
semiconductors which has not already been penetrated by
Western semiconductor firms. This market, we
estimate, will provide billions of dollars of semiconductor sales over the next decade.

Consumption of semiconductor devices in Eastern
Europe was about $400 million last year, and is expected
to increase to $1 billion annually by 1980. *

Assuming that U. S. -owned companies could capture
50 percent of the 1980 market, the East European sales
by U. S. -owned companies that year would be $500
million. This level can be realistically attained in the
Socialist countries by carefully negotiating agreements
which specify a market share in return for products and
technologies. Cumulative sales for the U. S. during 1974-
1980 time span would then be $2. 6 billion.

Should this East European business go to Japan,
however, we would find the $2. 6 billion addition to the
Japanese semiconductor industry representing 15
percent of their business for the remainder of the decade. [20]

In attempting to capitalize on this market opportunity, Hogan noted,

---

*Reproduced here as Table 5. 5.

TABLE 5.5

The Eastern European Semiconductor Market 1973-80

(Millions of U.S. dollars)

Product Line	1973	1974	1975	1976	1977	1978	1979	1980
Discrete semiconductors	248	276	310	333	353	356	348	344
Digital bipolar ICs	97	127	145	168	183	195	207	220
Linear ICs	23	29	42	55	70	88	110	136
MOS ICs	12	23	40	62	90	126	168	210
Hybrid ICs	20	25	33	42	54	65	77	90
Total	400	480	570	660	750	830	910	1,000

Source: Fairchild M. R. & P., Multinational Corporations and U.S. Foreign Policy, part 10, p. 386.

Fairchild has found it difficult to obtain a clear understanding of the Government's position on the transfer of technology—particularly semiconductor technology—to Eastern Europe.[21]

THE FAIRCHILD—UNITRA CASE

Hogan's experiences represent an important example of the export licensing problems associated with Eastern European sales of high-technology products. According to Hogan's testimony before the Church Multinational Subcommittee,

On February 1, 1973, Fairchild signed an agreement with Unitra of Poland, the foreign trade arm of the Polish Electronic Industry Association, to build a semiconductor production plant for the manufacture of devices for use only in commercial calculators. The plant was to employ what is known as P-MOS, or P-channel, metal-oxide-silicon technology. The agreement was signed at the apogee of detente, before certain doubts about this policy had been raised and before questions about technology transfers had become a topic of public debate.[22]

While not given assurances of export license approval by U.S. government officials, Fairchild was nevertheless encouraged to continue its negotiations.

According to Hogan,

> the agreement made good economic sense for Fairchild and for the United States. Fairchild was transferring relatively older semiconductor technology over a period of years so that it would not actually be in production use for 3 to 4 years. In addition, this technology—because of its general availability, its relative age, and certain specific provisions of the contract—would not create new competition for Fairchild or other U.S. semiconductor companies in their already established markets. Finally, the contract, in exchange for the transfer of technology, provided Fairchild with a guaranteed share of the future semiconductor market in Eastern Europe by granting to it one-half of all Unitra's purchases of silicon semiconductors for use in Poland. We predicted that this provision would result in tens of millions of dollars of U.S. exports to Poland over the course of this agreement. [23]

In short, Hogan felt both Fairchild and Unitra would derive mutual benefits from this venture. Fairchild estimated the agreement would create widespread employment spillovers. Some 1,500 man-years of additional labor would be required by Fairchild in its own domestic operations. Poland would be buying products and production technology which would not weaken present U.S. semiconductor production.

As Hogan summarized Fairchild's position in the Unitra case,

> Fairchild knew that the government would review its export license application regarding Unitra to judge how it affected national security. Fairchild did not have and never claimed to have all of the relevant facts. We presented our views to the government, stating that we believed the agreement would not adversely affect national security. But Fairchild was always aware that only the government could and should make the final decision in this matter. After all, a decision on Fairchild's application involved a number of major questions of policy obviously beyond the scope of Fairchild to answer:

- What are the various military uses and future needs for a particular semiconductor technology?
- What are Poland's technological and military capabilities?
- What relationship does Poland have with the Soviet Union and how would this affect the retransfer of semiconductor technologies and products?
- How would this agreement affect the Polish economy?
- What are the trade-offs of transferring sophisticated technology to an East European country against the political and economic advantages of increasing this type of trade?

These questions are obviously of significant scope. Indeed, they appear to be so complex and new that, faced with them, the government itself is just beginning to formulate relevant answers. [24]

To the disappointment of Hogan and other Fairchild executives,

Fairchild submitted an export license application for its Unitra contract to the Commerce Department on March 30, 1973. On June 28, 1974—15 months and several extensions of its Unitra contract later—the government made a decision to deny the license application. There was no way for Fairchild to know— in advance of that decision—whether the contract was or was not going to be approved. Indeed, it is ironic that after such lengthy, complex, frustrating, and expensive dealings with the Federal government on this matter, Fairchild still has no idea where the "line" is between acceptable and unacceptable agreements on the transfer of semiconductor technology to Eastern Europe. [25]

Given this result, Hogan's subsequent actions represent an invaluable input from a U. S. MNB.

Speaking as a spokesman for the Fairchild Corporation, Hogan tackled the export licensing problems he had encountered. He did this by playing devil's advocate and critic of U. S. government licensing procedures. He viewed the license-granting process as fragmented and lacking central direction.

The brunt of Hogan's criticism is aimed at the U. S. government's standard bureaucratic operating procedures. He believes that the

key problem is that the procedures by which an export
control license application are sent to various agencies
in the government and are then evaluated and decided
upon are vague and not publicly known. As you know,
the Export Administration Act is specifically exempted
from the Administrative Procedure Act. Thus, a
company like Fairchild, when making an application,
has to guess what the relevant considerations and
criteria are which the decision-makers will use. It
must even guess who those decision-makers are. Then
the company must, through a hit-or-miss, trial-and-error
process, locate those individuals, high and low in the
bureaucracy, who will be considering the license. This
is not open government; it is more than even closed
government. To us, it seems almost like hidden
government. [26]

In specific terms, Hogan felt the export licensing process
was devoid of a feedback mechanism. He and other Fairchild
officials, during the 15 months it took to process the license, never
received any clear explanations of any objections to the contract.
Indeed, rejection of the export license was made for general
reasons. According to Hogan,

This lack of feedback and this sense of frustration is
particularly troubling when viewed against the expense
for any company in participating in the "system." We
estimate that our key executives had to fly across the
country 20 times; our scientists devoted 50 man-months
to working on the proposal with the government. Over a
15-month period, Fairchild spent approximately $400
thousand on attempting to obtain government approval for
this agreement. It is hard to believe that such a long
and expensive process is required. Such costs will
probably deter smaller companies from embarking upon
major foreign agreements—a result which is both unfair
and anti-competitive. [27]

As a U.S. multinational businessman, Hogan's contribution
to clarifying this aspect of U.S. commercial policy cannot be
overlooked. Faced with the loss of a lucrative long-term contract,
the waste of at least $400,000 of the Fairchild Corporation's assets
spent on securing the license, and the remaining uncertainty as to
U.S. export licensing control procedures on high technology sales
to Eastern Europe, Hogan responded pragmatically. At great

expense to Fairchild but in an effort to balance U.S. policy makers'
views, Hogan counters the present ad hoc, case by case method
with an extensive alternative program. As noted in Appendix A
Hogan's input typifies the critical assistance U.S. MNBs can make.
His activist role is based on the belief that the export license control
process should be more orderly, more open, and more fair.

In sum, Hogan's criticism points to an ever-growing need for
executives and bureaucrats to be greater mutual contacts. Hopefully,
some of the inherent difficulties of controversial export license cases
might be resolved through enhanced cooperative bureaucrat-businessmen
interactions.

FUTURE U.S. INVESTMENT IN THE
SOVIET–BLOC ECONOMIES

As noted in Chapter 3, constitutional bars presently inhibit
equity investment in the Soviet Union and her Eastern European
allies. However, these prohibitations do not foreclose U.S. joint
venture and other cooperative commercial arrangements. For U.S.
MNBs and government officials, analysis of these industrial
cooperation agreements should be based upon two premises: geopolitics
and economic interdependence.

The primary premise concerns Eastern European geopolitics.
In spite of the basic uniformity of Soviet state socialism throughout
the Eastern bloc, great political differences exist between individual
countries. For example, in Poland, approximately 85 percent of the
farmland remains in private hands instead of state collectives. After
the United States, Poland has become the second most important
coal exporter. Edward Gierek, moderate leader of the Polish
United Workers Party, treats the Roman Catholic church with
all possible deference. Despite the atheist ideology of the
Communist Party, the PUWP, approximately 90 percent of
Poland's population remains Roman Catholic.

Czechoslovakia represents another diverse Eastern European
country. Rich in coal reserves, Czechoslovakia's highly developed
heavy industries are responsible for the high standard of living there.
In 1969, Gustav Husak replaced liberal Communist party leader
Alexander Dubcek. Since then, Husak has closely followed
Moscow's policies. Criticism of Husak's regime has been almost
totally suppressed. Today, seven years after Dubcek's overthrow,
punitive measures against him and his actual or suspected followers
remain in effect.

Other cases could be cited to describe the geopolitical diversity of the Eastern European bloc. These include Yugoslavia under Marshal Tito; Hungary, under Janos Kadar's leadership, where strong elements of a Western-style free market economy have been developed within the overall Communist structure; Ceaucescu's Romania, the only Communist nation with diplomatic ties to Israel; and Bulgaria or East Germany, both with close ties to the Soviet Union. Clearly, Eastern European geopolitical diversity must be considered an important factor in future cases of U. S. investment in the Soviet-bloc economies.

A second premise of concern to U. S. MNBs and policy makers focuses on increasing East-West economic interdependence. Dr. Wilfred Malenbaum, professor of economics at the University of Pennsylvania, has studied this subject by assessing the resource endowments of the United States, the Soviet Union, the People's Republic of China, and Japan. Commenting on Malenbaum's research, Dr. John P. Hardt, senior specialist in Soviet economics for the Library of Congress' Congressional Research Service, notes,

In any assessment of resource endowment the Soviet Union and the People's Republic of China (PRC) rank as countries with potentials for increased materials output and export, especially in energy and metals. The smaller socialist countries of East Europe and Asia do not have comparable resource endowment. Both the Soviet Union and the PRC need increasing material input for their industrialization processes (Table 5. 6) as do Western industrial nations such as the United States and Japan. [28]

Thus, U. S. MNBs and officials need to accept increasing East-West economic interdependence. More importantly, they must concern themselves with the policy implications of East-West economic interdependence.

Zbigniew Brzezinski, Herbert Lehman professor of Government and director, Research Institute of Communist Affairs, Columbia University, has analyzed numerous East-West economic problems. He looks at the problem of future, sustained, U. S. investment in the Soviet Union coupled with heavy Soviet indebtedness as a serious policy issue. Brzezinski's comments reveal that future U. S. investment with the Soviets mesh with the politics of detente:

TABLE 5.6

Demand for Materials, 1951-2000
(Unit per billion dollar gross domestic product)

	United States			Japan			U.S.S.R.			China	
	1951-55	1966-69	2000	1951-55	1966-69	2000	1951-55	1965-69	2000	1951-55	1966-69
Crude steel (metric ton million)	91	134	166	6	49	203	38	90	313	2	16
Iron ore (tons million)	59	75	141	3	40	161	28	71	215	2	15
Copper (metric ton thousand)	1,297	1,887	4,389	97	650	2.996	367	872	2,910	9	150
Zinc (metric ton thousand)	859	1,209	2,322	85	493	1,816	240	471	1,470	8	188
Fluorspar (metric ton thousand)	513	1,121	4,076	23	412	2,675	166	495	2,501	61	133
Sulfur (metric ton thousand)	5,246	8,712	26,648	1,242	2,006	7,490	*	2,853	10,920	*	1,157
Energy (coal equivalent million metric ton)	1,252	2,032	5,878	77	240	1,605	372	918	4,032	79	346

*Not available.

Source: Hardt, *Western Investment in Communist Economies*, U.S. Senate Committee on Foreign Relations, 93rd Cong., 2nd Sess., Committee Print (Washington, D.C.; Government Printing Office, August 5, 1974).

TABLE 5.7

USSR LOANS—EXIMBANK DIRECT AND UNGUARANTEED PRIVATE SOURCES, MARCH 1973 TO MARCH 1974

Russian Use	Russian Equity Sources (Private Unguaranteed)	Amount	Eximbank Direct	Total Project Cost	Beginning Date (Repayment)	Number of Years	Eximbank Interest Rate (Percent)
1. Tableware plant	$2,183,330 Bankers Trust (New York)	$ 9,824,850	$ 9,824,850	$21,833,000	Nov. 15, 1975	10	6
2. Piston manufacturing machinery	1,435,812 [a]	6,461,153	6,461,153	14,358,118	May 5, 1975	8	6
3. Iron ore pellet plant	3,600,000 [a]	16,200,000	16,200,000	36,000,000	May 20, 1977	8	6
4. Gas reinjection compressors	2,625,157 Wells Fargo (San Francisco)	11,813,204	11,813,204	16,251,565	Nov. 5, 1974	7	6
5. Piston manufacturing transline	1,572,204 French-American Bank Corp (New York)	7,074,919	7,074,919	15,722,042	May 5, 1974	8	6
6. Agricultural tractor part machine	600,000 Franklin National Bank (New York)	2,700,000	2,700,000	6,000,000	Nov. 5, 1975	8	6
7. Acetic acid plant	4,451,000 [a]	20,031,750	20,031,750	44,515,000	Feb. 10, 1979	10	6
8. Kama River truck plant	34,211,111 Chase Manhattan et al.	153,950,000	153,950,000	342,111,111	Oct. 10, 1977	12	6[b]7[c]
9. UFA motor works—flywheel transfer lines	745,810 [a]	3,356,145	3,356,145	7,458,100	Aug. 20, 1976	7	6
10. Ministry of Irrigation—canal-lining material	660,000 [a]	2,970,000	2,970,000	6,600,000	Dec. 15, 1975	5	6
11. Petrochemical industry—valve making machinery	470,000 [a]	2,115,000	2,114,000	4,700,000	Dec. 15, 1976	5	6
12. International trade center	8,000,000 Chase Manhattan (New York)	36,000,000	36,000,000	80,000,000	July 10, 1979	10	6
13. Circular knitting machines	562,000 Bankers Trust	2,529,000	2,529,000	5,620,000	Feb. 10, 1975	7	6
14. Tableware and dishware plant	689,314 Wells Fargo (San Francisco)	3,101,912	3,101,912	6,893,138	Mar. 10, 1976	10	6
15. Submersible electric pumping units	2,593,700 French-American et al.	11,671,650	11,671,650	15,937,000	Aug. 5, 1974	7	6
16. Fertilizer plants	40,000,000 Bank of America, et al.	180,000,000	180,000,000	400,000,000	May 20, 1979	12	6
Total		469,799,583	469,799,583				

[a] Not available.
[b] On $86,450,000.
[c] On $67,500,000.

Source: Senate staff report, *United States Trade and Investment in the Soviet Union and Eastern Europe*, p. 45.

It is for economists to judge whether in such a situation
the United States would find itself more dependent on
Soviet raw materials than the Soviet Union would on
American markets, but one can certainly conceive of a
Soviet leadership being tempted to use both its indebtedness
to the United States and American dependence on Soviet raw
materials for political ends. Moreover, the very scale
of Soviet indebtedness would, paradoxically, give the
Soviet leadership additional bargaining leverage. 29

Judging from Brzezinski's analysis, full-scale equity investment
in the Soviet Union and Eastern bloc economies run counter to present
Soviet ideology. However, Samuel Pisar, author of Coexistence and
Commerce, a comprehensive volume that describes the operational
and legal problems of East-West trade, believes, under certain
circumstances, U.S. investments can be made in the East.
According to Pisar,

Marx and Lenin said foreigners, let alone foreign
capitalists, cannot invest in a Communist country.
That's exploitation. All production must be state
owned. So it is futile to talk about owning an oil
refinery or gasification plant in Murmansk. But it
may not be impossible to build a plant under an agreement, transfer ownership to the appropriate Soviet
authority, and make a leaseback type of agreement to be
the effective operator in conjunction with the Soviet
authority. That doesn't offend the ideology.
    You can't acquire equity in a Soviet firm or sit on
a board of directors. But there is nothing to prevent
you from negotiating an elaborate contract which provides
for a management committee and a technical committee
responsible for designing, building and operating a
plant that would supply a need in the Soviet market and
manufacture for export.
    You can't have dividends or profit participations.
What you can have is royalty payment for patents or
know-how, engineering fees, management fees, interest,
selling commissions. None of this is precluded by Marx
and Lenin. There is nothing to prevent you from
incorporating a company outside the U.S.S.R. where
the equity is held 50-50 by an American company and
a Soviet enterprise. Such trans-ideological corporations
already exist. 30

Hardt's work provides evidence of Pisar's position. Hardt finds that Soviet leaders, seeking economic benefits, have accepted some of the political costs of East-West economic cooperation. Numerous cooperation agreements have been signed and equity investment has proceeded in Romania and Yugoslavia. As indicated in Table 5. 7 Soviet loans from the Export-Import Bank may be illustrative of the kinds of investments forthcoming throughout the Eastern bloc and the decades ahead.

Presently, Hardt sees industrial cooperation agreements as the forerunners of possible Soviet-bloc equity arrangements. He cites a recent report of the United Nations Economic Commission for Europe to substantiate this point. As Table 5. 8 demonstrates, based on a sample of 202 cases of East-West industrial cooperation, excluding Yugoslavia, in percentage terms, industrial cooperation agreements have varied. The agreements vary also by kind, including:

1. Licensing with payment in resultant products.
2. Supply of complete plants or production lines with payments in resultant products.
3. Coproduction and specialization.
4. Subcontracting.
5. Joint ventures.
6. Joint tendering or joint construction of similar projects. [31]

Each of these kinds of agreements varies significantly from the others. In Appendix B the types of cooperation arrangements are explained. In spite of the aftermath of the Jackson-Vanik Amendment to the 1973 Trade Bill, PL 93-618,

> a number of American firms are already assuming
> a practical role in some of the most important
> construction projects of the Ninth Five-Year Plan.
> Thus an agreement on technical collaboration and on
> the delivery of equipment for the Kama Automotive
> Plant for a total of $192 million has been concluded
> with Swindell-Dressler and certain other U. S. firms.
> Even new machinery is being delivered for construction
> projects in the oil and gas branches (contract with the
> Caterpillar firm to deliver equipment for laying large-
> diameter gas pipe). The agreement with International
> Harvester calls for the delivery of $40 million worth of
> construction machinery. Occidental Petroleum, the
> deal with which was mentioned above, will take part

TABLE 5.8

Distribution of East-West Industrial
Cooperation by Industrial Branches
(in percent)

	Total	Czecho-slovakia	Hungary	Poland	Romania	USSR
Chemicals	19.3	20.0	14.0	24.5	14.3	31.8
Transport equipment	17.3	26.7	20.9	11.3	28.6	13.6
Machine-tools	8.4	13.3	3.5	11.3	10.0	9.1
Mechanical engineering (excluding machine tools)	22.3	20.0	29.1	22.6	4.8	4.6
Electrical engineering and electronics	16.3	13.3	18.6	13.3	14.3	18.2
Others	16.4	6.7	13.9	17.0	28.0	22.7

Source: Hardt, Western Investment in Communist Economies, U. S. Senate, Committee on Foreign Relations, 93rd Cong., 2nd sess., Committee Print (Washington, D. C.: Government Printing Office, April 5, 1974).

in the construction of a large industrial complex for
the production of mineral fertilizer. The latter deal
is especially illustrative. Under the terms of the
agreement the American firm will deliver on a credit
basis to the Soviet Union the latest technology,
equipment, and the necessary supplies for the production
of mineral fertilizers. The credits will be repaid in the
form of deliveries of part of the finished product to the
USA after the entire enterprise has been put into
operation. The 20-year agreement guarantees both sides
a profit. The fulfillment of the agreement will give
USSR agriculture millions of additional tons of high-
quality fertilizer: 4 million tons of ammonium and
1 million tons of carbamide a year. [32]

The kinds of relationships developed by U.S. MNBs and U.S.
policy makers responsible for East-West investment issues will
play an important role in determining future U.S. investments in
the Soviet-bloc economies. Political, strategic, and financial
considerations will precede equity arrangements that may evolve
from present-day industrial cooperation agreements. Initiation and
implementation of these agreements rest heavily on the kinds of
support U.S. MNBs receive from legislators, bureaucrats, and
diplomats. The issues presented by U.S. investment in the Soviet-
bloc economies open a wide door for U.S. MNBs acting responsibly
to solidify U.S.-Soviet economic detente. U.S. MNBs can handle
the political risks associated with such investments if their efforts
are coordinated with U.S. government officials.

In the selected areas of East-West trade and investment
previously examined, U.S. MNBs play a role in the conduct of
U.S. foreign policy. For example, through the formal, indirect
means of manufacturer cooperatives, U.S. agricultural corporate
executives can shape and direct international commodity policies.
In the defense industries, a U.S. MNB like C. Lester Hogan provides
much-needed analysis and proposals for legislative remedies of
export licensing procedures on sales of high-technology goods in
the Eastern European bloc. These are just two examples of
multinational executive roles and East-West policies, the subject
of Chapter 6.

NOTES

1. U.S., Congress, House, Committee on Foreign Affairs, Global Scarcities in an Interdependent World, Hearings before the Subcommittee on Foreign Economic Policy, 93rd Cong., 2nd sess., May 1, 8, 9, 15, and 22, 1974, p. 232, hereafter cited as House Hearings, Global Scarcities.

2. Harold Geneen, "Feed the People," The New York Times, June 16, 1975, p. 27.

3. "Prices of Commodity Futures," The New York Times, August 12, 1975, p. 44.

4. U.S. Department of Agriculture, Foreign Agricultural Service, Trading with the USSR and Eastern Europe, by the Foreign Market Development and Evaluation Division, FAS M-264 (Washington, D.C.: Government Printing Office, June 1975), pp. 1-27, hereafter cited as FAS Study M-264.

5. U.S., Department of Agriculture, Foreign Agricultural Service, The Agricultural Situation in Eastern Europe, Review of 1974 and Outlook for 1975, by the European Area, Foreign Demand and Competition Division, Economic Research Service, Foreign Agricultural Economic Report No. 102 (Washington, D.C.: Government Printing Office, April 1975), pp. 10-12, hereafter cited as FAE Report No. 102.

6. Marshall I. Goldman, "The Russians are Buying," The New York Times, July 31, 1975, p. 27.

7. David M. Schoonover, "The Soviet Feed-Livestock Economy: Preliminary Findings on Performance and Trade Implications" in U.S., Department of Agriculture, Prospects for Agricultural Trade with the USSR, by the Foreign Demand and Competition Division, Economic Research Service, Joseph W. Willett, Director, ERS-Foreign 356 (Washington, D.C.: Government Printing Office, April 1974), p. 25, hereafter cited as ERS Report No. 356.

8. William Robbins, "Butz to Propose Grain Trade Plan," The New York Times, July 1, 1975, p. 18.

9. Robbins, p. 18.

10. Ibid.

11. David L. Hume, "Foreign Market Development—A Government/Industry Team" Foreign Agriculture 13, no. 21 (May 26, 1975):3.

12. Ibid.

13. Darwin Stolte, "Team Effort Boosts U.S. Farm Exports," Foreign Agriculture 13, no. 21 (May 26, 1975): 7-8.

14. U. S. , Congress, Senate, Committee on Foreign Relations, Multinational Corporations and United States Foreign Policy, Hearings before the Subcommittee on Multinational Corporations. 93rd Cong. , 2nd sess. , on Investment by Multinational Companies in the Communist Bloc Countries, June 17, 19, and July 17, 18, 19, and 22, 1974, Part 10 (Washington, D. C. : Government Printing Office, 1975), p. 223, hereafter cited as Multinational Corporations and United States Foreign Policy, Part 10.

15. Multinational Corporations and United States Foreign Policy, Part 10, p. 223.

16. Ibid. , pp. 240-41,

17. Ibid. , p. 241.

18. Ibid. , p. 360.

19. Ibid. , p. 361.

20. Ibid. , p. 386.

21. Ibid. , p. 360.

22. Ibid. , pp. 387-88.

23. Ibid.

24. Ibid. , p. 389.

25. Ibid.

26. Ibid. , p. 390.

27. Ibid. , p. 391.

28. U. S. , Congress, Senate, Committee on Foreign Relations, Subcommittee on Multinational Corporations, Western Investment in Communist Economies: A Selected Survey on Economic Interdependence, by John P. Hardt, George D. Holliday, and Young C. Kim, 93rd Cong. , 2nd sess. , Committee Print (Washington, D. C. : Government Printing Office, August 5, 1974), p. 11, hereafter cited as Hardt, Western Investment in Communist Economies.

29. Multinational Corporations and United States Foreign Policy, Part 10, p. 186.

30. Interview with Samuel Pisar in The Wall Street Journal, March 29, 1973, quoted in Hardt, Western Investment in Communist Economies, p. 30.

31. Hardt, Western Investment in Communist Economies, p. 35.

32. E. S. Shershnev, "Soviet–American Economic Relations at the New Stage," Soviet and Eastern European Foreign Trade 11, no. 1 (Spring 1975): 64.

6

MULTINATIONAL EXECUTIVE
ROLES AND EAST-WEST POLICIES

Dr. Daniel Bell, a professor of sociology at Harvard University, predicts the United States' development from 1975 to the year 2000 will create a postindustrial society. [1] In a postindustrial society, large numbers of white collar professionals in technical, government, university, and business fields will share overlapping planning roles. No longer would U.S. MNBs' concern be business. Instead, corporate citizenship would focus on broad-based societal needs. David Finn, chairman of the board of Ruder and Finn, argues that there already is a "need for businessmen to recognize that the refinement of business criticism into a respectable profession may prove to be the salvation of our economic and social system" [2] Thus, this book was undertaken as a study of business criticism. The research aim is to compare and contrast different perspectives on the role of U.S. MNBs within the nation's political system.

To find out what role U.S. MNBs play in the conduct of U.S. foreign policy on East-West trade and investment issues, the Fortune 500 population of U.S. MNCs was examined. [3] From this list, 30 corporations were chosen as the sample for this exploratory study. As noted in Chapter 2, the leading industrial, defense, and food corporations were contacted. The U.S. MNBs interviewed held a variety of positions. Three executives were corporate directors of international affairs. Four others were: a vice president of international affairs, a senior advisor on intergovernmental relations, a regional manager of international activities, and a coordinator for executive branch activities. A corporate vice president, a director of public relations, and a director of staff operations overseas complete the respondent set. All were personally interviewed in their offices. However, in one case, a director of staff operations overseas arranged a conference call for 90 minutes' duration to actively contribute to these findings.

U. S. government officials formed the remainder of the sample. As Table 2. 9, page 35, indicated, 25 government officials from 6 departments were confidentially interviewed. Of the government officials, 84 percent held GS ratings in the 13 to 15 category or above, the so-called supergrade ranks of senior U. S. government officials. Most bureaucrats categorized themselves as either administrators or communicators of East-West trade and investment policies. However, 11 of the 25 bureaucrats or 40 percent of those sampled, believed that they were formulators of East-West trade and investment policies.

EXECUTIVE-BUREAUCRATIC INTERACTIONS ON EAST-WEST
TRADE AND INVESTMENT ISSUES*

U. S. multinational business executives place a high priority on establishing long-term Eastern European export markets for U. S. manufactured goods and bulk agricultural commodities. They feel securing sales of technologically advanced U. S. products such as computers, wide-bodied aircraft, or semiconductors is also critical. However, the respondents did not clearly distinguish between the relative importance of promoting U. S. direct investment in Eastern Europe through joint ventures versus promotion of East-West detente as a U. S. government policy. Similarly, selling U. S. managerial expertise in Eastern Europe was usually mentioned as part of turnkey sales of technologically advanced U. S. products.

The sample of U. S. government officials evaluating East-West issues indicate a basic agreement with U. S. business executives. The mean score for 25 bureaucrats, 4. 36, is practically identical to the mean score of 4. 3 for the 10 U. S. MNBs. Unfortunately, due to unequal sample size, this similarity remains tentative. Yet a second point should be recognized. The 25 bureaucrats rated promoting East-West detente as a government policy almost as

---

*A complete data analysis is to be found in the author's "Entrepreneurial Politics: The Role of American Multinational Businessmen in the Conduct of U. S. Foreign Policy; A Case Study of East-West Trade and Investment Policies, " Ph. D. dissertation, George Washington University, 1976.

important as establishing long-term Eastern European export markets
for U.S. manufactured goods. However, U.S. government officials
believe promoting U.S. direct investment in Eastern Europe,
selling U.S. managerial expertise, and securing sales of high
technology products in the Soviet-bloc economies are all secondary
considerations to the goal of promoting East-West economic detente.

DIRECT, FORMAL PARTICIPATION OF U.S. MNBs IN EAST-WEST TRADE AND INVESTMENT ISSUES

When presented with East-West trade and investment issues of
concern to them, U.S. MNBs turn to a variety of U.S. government
departments for assistance. All the respondents had recent contact
with the State Department, especially the Bureau of Economic and
Business Affairs, and the Commerce Department, particularly the
Office of Export Administration. The other bureaus of the Commerce
Department were contacted by at least eight of the ten U.S. MNBs
interviewed. These were the Office of East-West Trade and the
Office of East-West Trade and Analysis. In addition, the Treasury
Department received the attention of at least six of the ten
respondents.

With the addition of the Department of Agriculture and the
Foreign Agricultural Service, all of the above departments
contacted by at least 60 percent of the MNBs were also contacted
by at least 18 to 25 bureaucrats. Yet, a much wider range of
intragovernmental units are involved in handling East-West trade
and investment issues. Nevertheless, the Departments of Commerce,
State, Agriculture, and the Treasury were contacted by 72 percent
of the bureaucrats interviewed. While the Defense Department is
brought in on East-West questions involving national strategic
importance, a wide host of government departments are inter-
connected by U.S. government officials handling East-West trade
and investment issues.

Often a U.S. government official in one department is in
personal contact through telephone, letter, or face-to-face meeting
with a counterpart official in another department. Most often,
State, Commerce, Treasury, or Agriculture Department officials
handle intra-agency East-West trade and investment issues. Both
the Commerce Department's Office of the Deputy Assistant Secretary
of East-West Trade and the Office of East-West Trade Analysis were
cited by over half the bureaucrats interviewed as handling their
East-West problems. The State Department's Office of East-West
Trade and the Commerce Department's Office of Export Administration were contacted by 10 of 25 bureaucrats on similar problems.

Based upon this data, the most frequent daily flow of intragovernmental contact on East-West trade and investment issues is between State and Commerce Department officials. U.S. MNBs with daily questions on East-West trade and investment policies have them handled by State or Commerce Department officials. Eight of ten U.S. MNBs stated that in the previous 12-month period, they had direct contact with the Departments of State, Commerce, or Treasury.

As Table 6.1 suggests, the nature of U.S. MNBs' contacts with U.S. government officials vary. All of the executives had telephone discussions with bureaucrats on technical points associated with the trade and sales of their products. Nine of the ten had face-to-face meetings with government officials to discuss East-West problems. In eight cases, the meetings included specific criticism of East-West trade policy and/or the exchange of advice between businessmen and bureaucrats. As noted in Table 6.2, 20 of the 25 officials stated that their contacts with MNBs included telephone calls

TABLE 6.1

Nature of MNBs' Contacts
(n=10)

Type of Contact	Percent of Sample Utilizing Type of Contact
Requests for general information on East-West trade	100
Requests for appointments with other government officials about East-West trade issues	90
Telephone conversations with MNBs on technical points	100
Face-to-face meetings with MNBs on technical points	90
Face-to-face meetings with MNBs to discuss East-West trade issues	70
Made as specific criticism of U.S. East-West trade policy	80
Professionally offered advice to U.S. MNB in the East-West trade field	80

Source: Jeffrey M. Brookstone, "Entrepreneurial Politics: The Role of American Multinational Businessmen in the Conduct of U.S. Foreign Policy; A Case Study of East-West Trade and Investment Politicies," Ph.D. dissertation, George Washington University, 1976, p. 282.

TABLE 6.2

Nature of U. S. Government Officials' Contacts
with U. S. MNBs
(n=25)

Type of Contact	Percent of Sample Utilizing Type of Contact
Requests for general information on East-West trade	76
Requests for appointments with other government officials about East-West trade issues	72
Telephone conversations with MNBs on technical points	80
Face-to-face meetings with government officials to discuss East-West trade issues	80
Face-to-face meetings with MNBs to discuss East-West trade issues	68
Made as specific criticism of U. S. East-West trade policy	60

Source: Data compiled by the author (see Table 6.1)

to discuss technical aspects of East-West trade policies. The same
number said they had face-to-face meetings with U. S. MNBs to
analyze these technical points. Of the bureaucrats sampled, 76 percent recalled MNBs requesting general information on East-West
trade and investment policies or offering the officials advice on these
policies. In contrast, 60 percent of the bureaucrats said they received
specific criticism of U. S. government East-West trade policy. This
criticism varied. It included demands for removal of export licensing
controls due to strategic considerations, complaints of the lack of
governmental support for trade promotion activities, and random
charges of encouraging the export of U. S. jobs and the sacrifice of
high technology patents.

Based upon the data collected for this exploratory study,
bureaucrats' contacts with U. S. MNBs representing the leading
industrial, defense, and food corporations do not appear widespread.
In general, most of the defense-related firms had more frequent
direct contact with the bureaucrats interviewed. As Table 6.3 indicates, 5 of these firms had contacted 8 of the 25 bureaucrats interviewed. One firm, Boeing, had contacted 12 of the 25 officials or
48 percent of the sample. In contrast, only 16 percent of the

bureaucrats interviewed had been contacted by any food corporation. The giant industrial MNCs appear to follow a low profile strategy. Only 7 of 25 bureaucrats had been contacted by corporations like General Motors, IBM, or Gulf Oil. As Table 6.4 indicates, U.S. MNBs minimize the exchange of information on these issues with business executives from corporations with whom they compete.

Nearly all the respondents (9 out of the 10 MNBs interviewed and all 25 bureaucrats) stated that at meetings of executives and bureaucrats held to discuss East-West trade and investment policies, policy differences had arisen. Table 6.5 shows 8 of 10 MNBs and 19 of the 25 bureaucrats categorized these differences as policy disagreements. In fact, 70 percent of the MNBs and 60 percent of the bureaucrats interviewed believed the policy differences involved a desire on

TABLE 6.3

Bureaucrats' Contact with U.S. MNCs
(n=25)

MNCs	Percent of Sample Having Contact with a Given MNC	MNCs	Percent of Sample Having Contact with a Given MNC
Exxon	20	McDonnell	
General Motors	28	Douglas	28
Ford Motor	12	TRW, Inc.	24
Texaco	8	General	
Mobil Oil	24	Dynamics	16
Standard Oil		Raytheon	12
of California	16	Wilson & Co.	
Gulf Oil	28	(LTV)	16
IBM	28	Esmark	8
ITT	24	Kraftco	4
Chrysler	16	Beatrice Foods	4
General Electric	32	Armour & Co.	
Western Electric	12	(Greyhound)	4
RCA	16	Borden	12
Rockwell		Ralston Purina	12
International	32	General Foods	16
United Aircraft	32	Coca-Cola	8
Lockheed	32	United Brands	8

Source: Data compiled by the author (see Table 6.1)

TABLE 6.4

MNBs' Contacts with Competitor MNCs
(n=25)

MNCs	Percent of Sample Contacting a MNC Other than Own	MNCs	Percent of Sample Contacting a MNC Other than Own
Exxon	20	United Aircraft	30
General Motors	30	Lockheed	20
Ford Motor	30	McDonnell Douglas	20
Texaco	10	TRW, Inc.	20
Mobil Oil	20	General Dynamics	20
Standard Oil		Raytheon	20
of California	0	Wilson & Co. (LTV)	0
Gulf Oil	10	Esmark	0
IBM	20	Kraftco	0
ITT	10	Beatrice Foods	0
Chrysler	20	Armour & Co.	
General Electric	60	(Greyhound)	0
Western Electric	10	Borden Co.	0
RCA	50	Ralston Purina	0
Rockwell		General Foods	0
International	10	Coca-Cola	10
Boeing	20	United Brands	0

Source: Data compiled by the author (see Table 6.1)

the part of U.S. MNBs to change U.S. government East-West trade and investment policies. Policy differences were resolved in two ways.

As indicated in Table 6.6, the primary method used to resolve policy differences involved U.S. MNBs reformulating their position to adapt to government policy. This method applied especially to the granting of export licenses required for foreign sales of high-technology products. For example, faced with a Defense Department refusal of export licenses for wide-bodied aircraft sales, U.S. executives were asked to remove strategic items, such as gyroscopes, from the planes. Afterward, the export licenses were granted.

A secondary method used to resolve policy differences involved bargaining. Three of ten executives believed there was some latitude of disagreement in their discussions with bureaucrats. This

TABLE 6.5

Source of Policy Differences

	Percent of Sample	
	MNBs	Bureaucrats
Type of Difference	(n=10)	(n=25)
Uncertainty as to the government's policy	20	44
Knowledge of the policy but disagreement with it	80	76
Desire on their part to change the government's policy	70	60
Disagreement with you as a government policy maker but not with the policy issue	10	12

Source: Data compiled by the author (see Table 6.1)

TABLE 6.6

Methods Used to Resolve Policy Differences

	Percent of Respondents	
	MNBs	Bureaucrats
Method	(n=10)	(n=25)
Reformulating your position	70	80
Accepting the U.S. government official's position	50	28
Lobbying for a change in the government's policy	50	44
Mutually compromising the policy differences	30	76

Source: Data compiled by the author (see Table 6.1)

TABLE 6.7

Activities Engaged in by Respondents in
Changing U. S. East-West Trade Policy

| | Percent of Respondents | |
| | MNBs | Bureaucrats |
Activities	(n=10)	(n=25)
Personally discuss the change with government officials	90	48
Present your views to government officials through information prepared by your corporation	60	80
Direct an advertising campaign or media campaign against the policy issue	20	24
Employ former government officials to express your views or contacted MNBs to express your views	60	52

Source: Data compiled by the author (see Table 6. 1)

flexibility permitted mutually agreed compromises to settle policy differences. Of 25 bureaucrats interviewed, 19, or 76 percent of the sample shown in Table 6. 6, believed policy differences were settled through this bargaining procedure. U. S. government officials consider bargaining a useful technique for resolving policy problems. However, the majority of U. S. MNBs felt U. S. government policy was fixed. U. S. MNBs felt lobbying activities with their congressional representatives a legitimate bargaining tool. As one executive stated, "Bureaucrats can't ignore Hill pressure."

As Table 6. 7 demonstrates, a variety of activities are engaged in by both U. S. MNBs and bureaucrats seeking to change East-West trade policy. Ninety percent of the U. S. MNBs interviewed said they personally discussed these changes with government officials in a direct, formal manner. The majority of MNBs rely on their own corporate information or former government officials employed by them to implement these changes. Fifty-two percent of the bureaucrats sampled said they had been contacted by MNBs. Of the 25 bureaucrats, 20 had presented their views to other government officials through information prepared for intradepartmental evaluation. This information was then presented to U. S. MNBs to explain

TABLE 6.8

Types of MNBs Contacting Government Officials
(n=25)

Types MNBs	Percent Contacted by Letter, Telephone, Telegram
Administrative-executive officers	84
External, government affairs types	44
PR, communication types	32
Financial officers	32
Marketing specialists	40

Source: Data compiled by the author (see Table 6.1)

why changes in East-West trade policy would or would not occur. As Table 6.8 indicates, high-level administrators, corporate executives, or marketing specialists received this information.

As noted in Table 6.9, former civil servants frequently accept positions with U.S. MNCs. For example, after four years as undersecretary of the treasury for monetary affairs, Jack F. Bennett recently resigned his position stating, "I am broke."[4] He rejoined his former company, Exxon. Former cabinet officials such as Treasury Secretary George Schultz and H.E.W. Secretary Caspar Weinberger have joined the Bechtel Corporation. As Table 6.10 notes, seven of ten MNBs believed former government officials are useful in presenting their corporations' needs. Yet, once they are

TABLE 6.9

Former Government Officials Employed by MNCs
(n=10)

Types	Percent of Sample
Congressmen and/or senators	30
Civil servants: GS 15 and above	50
Military: rank of captain or above	40

Source: Data compiled by the author (see Table 6.1)

TABLE 6.10

Contribution of Former Bureaucrats
page130   According to Mutlinational Businessmen

(n=10)

Contribution is:	Percent of Sample
Critically essential to effecting changes in East-West trade policy	50
Generally useful in presenting their companies' needs	70
Marginal, intangible assistance in influencing U.S. East-West trade policy	70
Of little significance in effecting policy changes	60

Source: Data compiled by the author (see Table 6.1)

out of the government, former bureaucrats may offer their corporation marginal, intangible assistance in influencing East-West trade policy. Similarly, former officials may have little impact on effecting policy changes. Indeed, as Table 6.11 depicts, bureaucrats believe the contribution of MNBs, including former bureaucrats who are now MNBs, is one of adequately presenting their corporations' needs. Bureaucrats find MNBs contribute little of significance in effecting East-West trade and investment policy changes. Yet 20 of 25 bureaucrats believed U.S. MNBs' contribution was an intangible operational assistance. This operational assistance influenced U.S. government East-West trade policy such as export control.

Of 25 government officials, 23 believed their contacts with U.S. MNBs permitted MNBs to directly and formally participate in the conduct of U.S. foreign policy. In reference to influencing East-West trade policy, the diversity of comments from bureaucrats about U.S. MNBs' activities indicate such activities are legitimate, necessary, and helpful. For example, a USDA official who recently served as a U.S. agricultural attache in Moscow noted that, "Sales executives know the top officials. Many contacts with the trade analysis people exist." A Commerce Department trade specialist finds that the goal of U.S. MNBs is to sell in Eastern Europe. He stated, "The companies know what the problems are. They must conform to what the policies are. To effect policy changes, the big guns make their wishes known to legislative bodies." Several State Department

officials verified these comments, adding, "Policy is not merely a
piece of paper."

U. S. MNBs initiate many formal, direct contacts with bureaucrats. While some rely on local Washington representatives to present their views, others like David Rockefeller, Chase Manhattan's
global banker, move through the Eastern European countries like
quasi-government officials. In general, bureaucrats contacted by
U. S. MNBs felt the businessmen suffered from an unfair stereotype.
Twenty-four bureaucrats believed the uniformity of performance of
U. S. MNBs was a highly cooperative one. However, one FSO believed
this input should be directed exclusively at congressional representatives.

Six of the MNBs interviewed felt they directly and formally
participated in the conduct of U. S. foreign policy. One U. S. auto
executive stated, "Executive-diplomat exchanges are especially
helpful. Without question, these exchanges are bound to be helpful
to industry." Such exchanges permit wider U. S. MNB-bureaucrat
contact for mutual benefit. As one oil executive related, "We don't
conduct our business as an adjunct of U. S. foreign policy. If our
business has benefit for government policy, fine. In the East-West
trade area, government policy acts as a limiting constraint on our
business operations. Our contacts with government officials ·allow
us to better appreciate what the policy will be. We are constantly

TABLE 6.11

Contribution of MNBs Evaluated by Bureaucrats
(n=25)

Contribution is:	Percent of Bureaucrats Sample
Critically essential to effecting changes in East-West trade policy	72
Generally useful in presenting their companies' needs	92
Marginal, intangible assistance in influencing U. S. East-West trade policy	80
Of little significance in effecting policy changes	88

Source: Data compiled by the author (see Table 6.1)

involved in many long-term negotiations so it would be unrealistic for us not to participate directly in U. S. policy questions. "

DIRECT, INFORMAL PARTICIPATION OF U. S. MNBs IN EAST-WEST TRADE AND INVESTMENT ISSUES

Through the use of intermediaries and nongovernmental organizations, U. S. MNBs participate in a direct, informal manner in U. S. foreign policy. Acting on behalf of a multinational businessman, the intermediary will contact a U. S. government official to clarify the status of an export license, inquire about the nature of East-West trade policy toward a particular country, or advocate a position such as granting most-favored-nation status to Romania. As featured in Table 6.12, a variety of intermediaries are utilized for such tasks. There are two high-frequency types of intermediaries. The first are host government embassy officials, especially commercial attache officers. The second type of intermediary is the international lawyer. Those who specialize in East-West trade problems are particularly active as intermediaries.

U. S. MNBs emphasized the importance of developing direct contacts with the U. S. official closest to their specific problem. When this is not possible, intermediaries are employed. Bureaucrats are generally receptive to such intermediaries. For example, often the U. S. Chamber of Commerce was cited as such an effective nongovernmental organization. Another organization, The Atlantic

TABLE 6.12

MNBs' Intermediaries Utilized for Direct, Informal Participation in U. S. Foreign Policy

	Percent of Sample Contacted	
	MNBs	Bureaucrats
Type of Intermediary	(n=10)	(n=25)
A former U. S. government official	20	48
A host government embassy official	90	80
Another MNC's business executive	20	44
An international lawyer specializing in East-West trade	70	64

Source: Data compiled by the author (see Table 6.1)

TABLE 6.13

Groups Used by U. S. MNBs to Effect Changes
in U. S. Government Export Licensing Policy

	Percent of Sample	
	MNBs	Bureaucrats
Groups	(n=10)	(n=25)
Congressmen and/or senators	30	76
Foundations	30	36
Nonprofit organizations	20	28
Study groups	50	24
Party officials	20	40
Trade associations	80	84
Other	20	8

Source: Data compiled by the author (see Table 6.1)

Council of the United States, focuses on policy questions. Henry H.
Fowler, former Secretary of the Treasury, serves as chairman of
the Atlantic Council. Other distinguished public servants, including
General Lauris Norstad, Eugene V. Rostow, and former Commerce
Secretary Alexander B. Trowbridge serve as vice chairmen. Members
of the Atlantic Council Steering Committee on East-West Trade,
including Willis C. Armstrong and Philip H. Trezise, both former
Assistant Secretaries of State for Economic Affairs, handle U. S.
MNBs' inquiries into the long-term direction and scope of East-West
trade and investment policies. However, if a U. S. MNB's request
focuses on daily concerns, he will employ an intermediary private
consulting firm. Firms like Robert Nathan Associates or WJS Incorporated specialize in East-West trade and investment problems.
Bureaucrats interviewed for this study noted these two firms as frequently acting in behalf of U. S. MNBs.

Sometimes U. S. MNBs utilize several different kinds of groups
to influence bureaucrats responsible for changing U. S. government
export licensing policies. As seen in Table 6.13, U. S. MNBs rely
heavily on trade associations to represent their views. Organizations
like the Aerospace Industries Association, the Electronic Industries
Association, the U. S. Feed Grains Council, and the U. S. Chamber
of Commerce function as effective trade associations. In other
instances, research organizations like the Brookings Institution or
the American Enterprise Institute will present a study group report

commissioned by U. S. MNBs. Several executives mentioned studies done by ECAT. Chaired by Donald M. Kendall, chief executive officer of Pepsico, Inc. , ECAT's recent study entitled The Multinational Corporation: American Mainstay in the World Economy was cited as the kind of research used by business executives to inform bureaucrats and the U. S. public. A Boeing executive described another intermediary—the academician. Interested in understanding the legal complexities of U. S. export licensing policies and procedures to Eastern Europe, Boeing hired Samuel Pisar. Pisar, author of Coexistence and Commerce, conducted seminar training programs for Boeing's multinational executives. In short, eight of ten U. S. MNBs thought the intermediaries they utilized proved helpful to fulfilling their requests. The same number of MNBs believed they were changing the conduct of U. S. foreign economic policy by seeking changes in the export licensing program. As one oil corporation senior advisor for international relations stated, "We sometimes use intermediary business agents to facilitate normal business procedures. They help us focus the issues and best organize our global resources on a particular set of trade policy questions. This is part of our day-to-day business activity. "

U. S. government officials mentioned they had been contacted by a host of different trade associations. These included the National Machine Tool Builders, the National Coal Association, the American Pharmaceutical Association, the American Petroleum Institute, and the National Association of Manufacturers (NAM). Other groups, such as the East-West Trade Council, the U. S. Feed Grains Council, the Farm and Industrial Equipment Institute, follow East-West trade issues carefully. Of the 25 bureaucrats interviewed, 19 cited specific congressional inquiries transmitted to them by U. S. MNBs. These MNBs sought clarification of export licensing policies or desired to resolve their particular operational problem through congressional intercession. In a majority of cases, bureaucrats were able to provide a helpful outcome for the multinational executives' requests.

Among the bureaucrats sampled, Table 6.14 indicates that 84 percent believed MNBs were changing the conduct of U. S. foreign economic policy by seeking changes in the export licensing program. U. S. MNBs' participation in government policy making varied considerably. A Commerce Department official said, "Small businessmen think they are international executives. They want to advise the Government. Executives from big MNC know how things are done. They contact the specific line, department and person in charge of their problem. " Indeed, intermediary and nongovernmental organizations specialize in helping U. S. MNBs learn the proper political channels. One State Department official noted wryly, "Policies change but the bureaucracy doesn't. " Consequently, to clarify export

TABLE 6.14

MNBs Influencing Export Licenses

	Percent of MNBs (n=10)	Percent of Bureaucrats (n=25)
Utilized and was contacted by intermediary	80	88
Found intermediary helpful in fulfilling MNB's requests	80	52
Believed intermediary was utilized to change export licensing program	75	84

Source: Data compiled by the author (see Table 6.1)

licensing policies, bureaucrats are called upon for assistance. Unfortunately, according to a USDA official, "The letters we receive about grain export problems indicate a great deal of public misinformation about these problems. Most writers think the Government is giving the grain away. They don't realize private traders, not the Government, are trading the grain. Producers are trying to export it." This lack of public understanding explains the value U.S. MNBs place in employing intermediaries to seek changes in U.S. government export licensing policies.

Table 6.15 indicates that businessmen and bureaucrats are interested in changing selected U.S. government East-West investment policies. U.S. MNBs favor influencing investment policies chiefly through trade associations. Multinational executives cited groups like the National Export Managers Association, the U.S./USSR Trade Council, and the East-West Trade Council as examples of such trade associations. In all cases, American business executives emphasized that long-term Eastern European investment was judged on a case-by-case basis. A Gulf Oil executive stated that his corporation had been sought out by Soviet and Romanian trade delegations. However, before Gulf would commit itself to Eastern European investments, Gulf would have to be provided with tax or depreciation incentives. Thus, eight of ten MNBs felt that through the use of intermediaries, especially trade associations, multinational executives are permitted to influence the conduct of U.S. foreign economic policy in the area of Eastern European direct investments. U.S. MNBs felt

TABLE 6.15

MNBs Influencing East-West Investment Policies

Percent of Sample:	Percent of MNBs (n=10)	Percent of Bureaucrats (n=25)
feel U. S. government policy permits joint ventures to occur	100	84
believe MNBs seek changes in U. S. government East-West investment policies	70	76
believe MNBs' requests for changes of East-West investment policies are helpful	60	68
feel MNBs were changing conduct of U. S. foreign economic policy through changes in Eastern European direct investment policies	80	80

Source: Data compiled by the author (see Table 6.1)

trade councils are taking the initiative in opening up Eastern Europe to long-term U. S. investment. Presently, the trade councils' focus emphasizes Export-Import Bank credits for Soviet sales and MFN status for Romania. The U. S. Chamber of Commerce now provides the major source of current information on U. S. investment in Eastern Europe. In fact, three respondents praised two of the chamber's publications by name. [5]

Of 25 bureaucrats interviewed, 20 believed the U. S. MNBs' input in changing U. S. government Eastern European investment policy originated in trade association activities. As noted in Table 6.16, more than half of the bureaucrats received congressional or senatorial requests prompted by U. S. MNBs. As constituents, business executives make requests of bureaucrats based on information the MNBs receive from the NAM, the Agricultural Trade Association, or a number of newsletters published by multinational banks. First National City's, Morgan Guaranty Trust's, and Chase Manhattan's newsletters reach a wide and influential audience of U. S. MNBs. Three State Department officials emphasized that U. S. business executives often load up on critical information about Eastern Europe's political situation before leaving to evaluate joint venture or licensing opportunities. Upon their return, U. S. executives not only understand the long-run investment opportunities in the Eastern bloc but are willing to exchange their views with congressmen. Thus, even though current U. S. policy emphasizes direct sales but not direct investment in the Eastern bloc, 7 of the 10 MNBs interviewed and 21 of the 25 bureaucrats believed that intermediaries and nongovernmental organizations permit U. S. MNBs to participate formally but indirectly in the conduct of U. S. government Eastern European export licensing and investment policies.

For U. S. MNBs, intermediary and nongovernmental organizations function as useful groups. These groups supplement U. S. MNBs' direct contacts with U. S. government officials. Through intermediaries, executives often find out what is official U. S. government policy. U. S. MNBs in disagreement with U. S. government East-West trade and investment policies can contact fellow trade association members to lobby for reevaluation of these policies. For example, a group such as the National Machine Tool Builders' Association provides its membership with an overview of the governmental policy problems affecting its members. As sellers of high-technology machine tools, individual tool builders utilize this information to improve their operating strategies in the Eastern European markets. Through intermediaries and nongovernmental organizations, U. S. MNBs locate market opportunities and forecast the direction of East-West trade policies.

TABLE 6.16

Groups Used by U. S. MNBs to Effect Changes in U. S. Government
Investment Policy in Eastern Europe

	Percent of Sample	
	MNBs	Bureaucrats
Groups	(n=10)	(n=25)
Congressmen and/or senators	30	52
Foundations	20	20
Nonprofit organizations	20	8
Study groups	20	16
Party officials	30	20
Trade associations	50	80
Other	20	—

Source: Data compiled by the author (see Table 6.1)

INFORMAL, DIRECT PARTICIPATION OF U. S. MNBs
IN EAST-WEST TRADE AND INVESTMENT ISSUES

U. S. MNBs analyzing Eastern European export licensing and direct investment issues soon find that a small number of bureaucrats concentrate of these policy questions. According to Table 6.17, few working relationships between multinational executives and bureaucrats are derived from informal school, family, or elite club ties. For MNBs, direct professional ties often lead to social contact or acquaintanceship ties with U. S. government officials. Professional groups such as the Retired Officers Association or the Society of Automotive Engineers provide only infrequent professional friendships with bureaucrats. G. William Domhoff, professor of psychology at the University of California, has described an elaborate multinational businessmen's social club, the Bohemian Club of San Francisco. [6] In this study, only three bureaucrats referred to any informal ties with U. S. MNBs. An FSO provided an explanation for the lack of such ties. In practice, State Department officials do not remain in one position for very long. The FSOs rotate frequently and are forced to be quite mobile. Additionally, FSOs and other bureaucrats are recruited from a highly diverse background. Yet, MNBs find they have some similarity in background with the bureaucrats they contact. U. S. MNBs find background ties help them to participate in the conduct of East-West trade policies in an informal and direct manner.

A higher percentage of MNBs (9 out of 10) believed their backgrounds were similar to those of bureaucrats than the reverse (19 bureaucrats out of 25). Table 6.18 indicates that several factors explain the background similarity between bureaucrats and MNBs

TABLE 6.17

MNBs' Informal, Direct Ties with Bureaucrats

Ties	Percent of Sample Identifying Tie	
	MNBs (n=10)	Bureaucrats (n=25)
Elite club ties	—	8
School ties	—	12
Family ties	—	8
Professional ties	50	8

Source: Data compiled by the author (see Table 6.1)

TABLE 6.18

Factors Promoting Similarity of Background
between Bureaucrats and U. S. MNBs

Similarity of Background based on:	Percent of Sample Citing Factor	
	MNBs (n=10)	Bureaucrats (n=25)
past government-related employment	50	52
past business-related experience	60	52
military service	30	—
similar education	60	25
similar personal goals	30	16
community involvement	50	64
coincident, random factors	20	12

Source: Data compiled by the author (see Table 6.1)

working in the East-West trade area. For example, educational training, past business and prior government employment provided an indirect experiential tie between MNBs and U. S. government officials. In addition, both groups indicated that their involvement in community groups including athletic, country, and men's clubs provided a basis for common social background. Other factors, such as overseas residence, attendance at government-sponsored executive-diplomatic seminars and/or membership in academic groups like the American Economic Association typified the kinds of informal ties between U. S. MNBs and bureaucrats. One State Department official categorized these informal ties as information conduits. In other words, because the Foreign Service is composed of a relatively small group of 30,000, plus officials stationed in more than 140 foreign countries, informal personal ties between diplomats and multinational executives serve two purposes. Primarily, informal ties lead to information transmission from overseas missions to the State Department in Washington. Second, by cultivating these ties, FSOs can frequently predict market trends or host country political developments.

Table 6.19 lists the percentage of bureaucrats and businessmen who believe that informal ties, such as family or background similarity, permit U. S. MNBs to participate informally and directly in East-West trade policies. However, five of ten executives thought that

TABLE 6.19

MNBs' Participation in East-West Trade Policies—
Informal, Direct Ties

Respondent Groups	Percent of Sample*		
	Yes	No	Don't know
MNB (n=10)	50	50	—
Bureaucrats (n=25)	68	28	4

*Stating informal ties facilitated U. S. MNBs' participation in
U. S. foreign economic policy
Source: Data compiled by the author (see Table 6.1).

policies involving export licenses or joint venture cooperative agreements with Eastern European Socialist countries would be handled on
a case-by-case straight business basis. In these instances, the merits
of East-West trade policies would be judged strictly on the basis of
present-day corporate profitability. Yet a defense contractor related
that informal ties prove useful to him. These ties lead to invitations
to dinners and luncheons essential for establishing additional business
contacts in the East-West field.

Some bureaucrats discounted the effects informal U. S. MNBs'
ties played on East-West outcomes. These bureaucrats argued that
businessmen and government officials maintain separate and distinct
perceptions of East-West trade policies. In addition, these bureaucrats believed U. S. executives worry more about how to implement
policies or operationalize them than about the formulation of substantive policy inputs. Despite this view, the majority of U. S. government
officials found background similarities with multinational executives
essential. For example, a USDA official noted that many multinational agribusinessmen had served as administrators in the FAS.
Clifford Hardin, former Secretary of Agriculture, is currently a
Ralston Purina vice president. Multinational executives like Hardin
understand how East-West policies are implemented and changed
within the bureaucracy.

Informal, direct participation by U. S. MNBs in East-West
trade policies remains a pragmatic process. A Department of
Defense official commented, "Multinational executives understand as
much policy as they want to and just enough to get the job done. None
of them want to go to jail. Consequently, their personal relationships
are especially discreet." Clearly, MNBs don't make policy. Executive

branch officials fulfill this responsibility. Because U. S. multinational businessmen have open access to U. S. officials, some entrepreneurs like Armand Hammer or David Rockefeller can pursue careers as frustrated diplomats. In these cases, the U. S. MNBs' personal ties to bureaucrats are publicly identifiable. Through a mixture of self-interest in global profit opportunities, the Hammers and Rockefellers practice operating strategies which implement East-West economic detente.

INFORMAL INDIRECT PARTICIPATION OF U. S. MNBs IN EAST-WEST TRADE AND INVESTMENT ISSUES

In the past, U. S. MNBs attempted to defeat the Jackson-Vanik Amendment to the 1973 Trade Bill, PL 93-618. In this area, U. S. MNBs sought to influence the conduct of U. S. foreign policy involving East-West trade issues through organized public opinion appeals. These mass appeals are the informal, indirect means U. S. MNBs employ to influence U. S. policy makers. The most common appeal is the full page newspaper ad. It is usually placed in key papers including The Wall Street Journal, The New York Times, The Washington Post, or The Journal of Commerce. Both businessmen and bureaucrats also find public opinion appeals in such widely read business magazines as Business Week, Fortune, or Commerce Today. Although Washington bureaucrats rely on cables, congressional inquiries, and columnists such as Joseph Kraft or Jack Anderson for news or current public opinion shifts on East-West trade issues, with few exceptions, bureaucrats and MNBs find public opinion campaigns helpful to East-West trade policy development. In particular, educational and informative feature articles on the Eastern European bloc nations alert U. S. executives to overseas marketing opportunities. Unfortunately, public opinion appeals insufficiently explain the links between domestic economic policy matters and U. S. foreign policy requirements.

U. S. government officials strongly believe that the individual points of view presented in organized public opinion appeals serve a vital function. For short time periods, mass appeals direct the attention of bureaucrats to critical East-West trade issues. This permits government officials to respond to the appeals through intra-governmental policy statements or press releases. More than 90 percent of the multinational executives and bureaucrats interviewed believe organized public opinion appeals permit MNBs to participate informally and indirectly in the conduct of East-West trade policies. An aerospace executive emphasized that public appeals on behalf of the MNCs need to be made, that reports like the ones done for ECAT must funnel down to the grassroots, and that people need to know that U. S. executives are creating jobs, not eliminating them. In short, organized public opinion appeals provide a channel easily utilized by U. S. MNBs. As one State Department official demanded, "There is a need for massive public education on the contributions of American multinational executives. Unions have their own perspectives on these contributions. But Congress is impressed by wide constituencies. Informal, indirect participation of American MNB in East-West trade issues should allow business to counterbalance the impact of unions. It is American MNB who are making the theme of economic inter-dependence workable."

THE ROLES MNBs PLAY IN THE CONDUCT OF
U. S. FOREIGN POLICY

Respondents were asked to rank by order of importance the roles U. S. MNBs play in the conduct of U. S. foreign policy. As defined in Chapter 1, five roles were designated. These included a direct, formal role; a formal, indirect role; an informal, direct role; an informal, indirect role and a role of no participation for U. S. MNBs in East-West trade and investment policies. These role types were evaluated by each respondent on a scale of one to five. The respondent gave the highest ranking, "5," to the role he believed MNBs presently play in the U. S. foreign policy process.

Bureaucrats and U. S. MNBs were in close agreement with the two formal roles U. S. MNBs play in the conduct of U. S. foreign

TABLE 6.20

Roles MNBs Feel They Play in U. S. Foreign Policy
(n=10)

Role	Number of MNBs Selecting Role	Percent of Sample
Informal, indirect	1	10
Informal, direct	0	—
Formal, indirect	3	30
Formal, direct	4	40
No participation	2	20

Source: Data compiled by the author (see Table 6.1)

TABLE 6.21

Roles Bureaucrats Feel MNBs Play in U.S. Foreign Policy
(n=25)

Roles	Number of Bureaucrats Selecting Role	Percent of Sample
Informal, indirect	2	8
Informal, direct	3	12
Formal, indirect	5	20
Formal, direct	14	56
No participation	1	4

Source: Data compiled by the author (see Table 6.1).

policy. The direct, formal role received the highest mean score from both respondent groups. Defense, Commerce, and State Department officials believed this role particularly critical. The individual means for these departments, respectively 5.0, 4.4 and 4.2, indicate this point. The direct, informal role, or participation of MNBs through intermediaries and nongovernmental organizations in East-West trade policies, received the second highest mean score from both groups. In the case of the Department of Agriculture, these intermediaries include the agricultural cooperator programs.

The two informal roles were evaluated differently by each group. Bureaucrats placed the informal, direct role involving ties between MNBs and U.S. government officials ahead of the informal, indirect role involving organized public opinion appeals. With one exception, bureaucrats believed U.S. MNBs had a legitimate role to play in the conduct of U.S. foreign policy.

U.S. MNBs didn't significantly differentiate between the two informal roles open to them. They marginally favored the use of public opinion appeals instead of personal ties to government officials as a means of participating in East-West trade and investment policies. Three of the ten executives interviewed believed U.S. MNBs should play no participative role in the conduct of U.S. foreign policy. These respondents represented corporations who adopted a low-profile external relations strategy. Thus, as Tables 6.20 and 6.21 indicate, 70 percent of the MNBs and 76 percent of the bureaucrats interviewed believed the two formal roles were the most appropriate ones. These roles permitted U.S. MNBs' formal input into U.S. foreign policy covering East-West trade and investment issues.

Individual respondents were asked if their highest ranked role was the role they wanted U.S. MNBs to play. No role conflict arose among multinational executives and role conflict was indicated by only 2 of 25 U. S. government officials. In general, U. S. MNBs felt the formal, direct role allowed for the broadest contact and support of U. S. government policies. MNBs represent a source of vast information which government policy makers frequently need to determine policy. Transmission of this information by corporate executives directly to bureaucrats offers the widest opportunity for mutually acceptable results. However, one oil company executive adamantly refused any participative role in East-West trade and investment policy determination. He declared, "I wouldn't call up Kissinger and seek his help. I would have no influence at all. I must deal in political realities. Foreign policy issues are too complex for us to capitalize on them. Fortunately, we don't run the Government or the world. We accept our goofs and hold ourselves responsible for mistakes we make with foreign governments."

Bureaucrats offered a diversity of responses to explain their highest-rank role choices. For example, those who favored the direct, formal role for U. S. MNBs believed that a multinational businessman with an operational or substantive policy problem deserves the clearest, quickest and most responsible direct response possible from policy makers. If the multinational businessman's view is based on facts and raises reasonable national policy questions, as an Executive Office official commented, "We desire that viewpoint. Direct views should flow through business-organized channels into the bureaucracy. Those views should be exchanged in as direct a way as possible."

Several bureaucrats preferred MNBs to participate in U. S. foreign policy in a formal, indirect manner. These bureaucrats indicated trade associations can be quite valuable to the policy maker. One State Department official stated, "The informality of the American business community is its greatest strength. We can't make policy in the dark. MNB give us feedback. They let us know what we should be seeing. This leads to policy harmonization. Realistically, policy-makers decide issues incrementally or in component sections. Recommendations received from outside the bureaucracy allow decisions on East-West trade and investment policies to reflect the needs of American MNB." Another official, a Commerce Department analyst, noted the importance of a formal, indirect contribution from U. S. MNBs. He remarked, "It gives the MNB a chance to set forth his opinions. They provide for a meeting of minds. Sometimes the MNB's opinions are better than policy. Sometimes the reverse. But his input is essential for a meeting of minds in the policy area."

In a highly specialized field such as bulk agricultural commodity trading, the U. S. MNB must rely on personal ties to U. S. government officials to keep up with fast-changing policy developments. An informal, direct participatory role then occurs. For example, a

USDA official stated, "The agricultural economists in the Foreign Agricultural Service know each other. It's like a ministry of agriculture. It's quite informal. There are visits between agricultural economists and American MNB here and abroad. The performance of the multinational businessman is keyed to his MNC. When the company's interest conflicts with national interest in the short run, personal ties between officials and executives resolve these conflicts." Another Agriculture Department official said, "We assist everybody equally. However, we would rather have the proposal come from a trade association. They represent more than one company and we know of their related members."

Other bureaucrats favored MNBs' participation in U.S. foreign policy in an indirect, informal form. A State Department FSO said that there should be a distance between policy makers and MNBs. "They have separate responsibilities and interests to represent. Public opinion keeps them separated." A USDA official believed U.S. MNBs should use organized public opinion appeals because "Foreign policy and commercial policy go hand in hand. We must have trade policy linked with foreign policy for our self-preservation. Only appeals to the public can get this point across."

NOTES

1. Daniel Bell, The Coming of the Post-Industrial Society: A Venture in Social Forecasting (New York: Basic Books, Inc., Publishers, 1973), pp. ix-489.

2. David Finn, "The Business of Businessmen is Not Just Business," The New York Times, June 28, 1975, p. 27.

3. Bro Uttal, "The Fortune Directory of the 500 Largest Industrial Corporations," Fortune 91, no. 5 (May 1975): 208-35.

4. "Treasury Official Quits, Cites His Money Woes," The New York Times, June 19, 1975, p. 49.

5. See Chamber of Commerce of the United States, The Climate for Investment Abroad (Washington, D.C.: Chamber of Commerce, September 1974), pp. 1-109, and Romanian-U.S. Economic Council, U.S. Section, Chamber of Commerce of the United States, Romanian-U.S. Joint Ventures: Background for Implementation (Washington, D.C.: Chamber of Commerce, November 1974), pp. 1-64.

6. G. William Domhoff, "Playgrounds of the Powerful: How Fat Cats Keep in Touch," Psychology Today 9, no. 3 (August 1975): 44-48.

7

SUMMARY
AND CONCLUSIONS

The general objective of this research effort was to describe
and explain the role U. S. multinational businessmen play in the
conduct and implementation of U. S. foreign policy in the East-West
trade and investment field. Specifically, interest focused on the
following factors:

1. The role U. S. government officials believed U. S. MNBs
played in the conduct of U. S. foreign policy in the area of East-
West trade and investment.
2. The role U. S. MNBs believed they fulfilled in the conduct
of U. S. foreign policy.
3. The differences which emerged between U. S. government
officials and multinational businessmen over the role U. S. multinational businessmen play in the conduct of U. S. foreign policy
in the area of East-West trade and investment.

The main research findings related to these objectives
are summarized below:

1. Multinational business executives' political roles and
activities are determined by reference and peer group pressure.
The political roles include: (a) a direct role as private foreign
policy makers, (b) an unintended direct role as instruments of
influence, and (c) an indirect role as agenda formulators of U. S.
foreign policy priorities. Reference and peer group pressures
include: (a) the self-identity, aspirations, and values a multinational
businessman derives from other MNBs with whom he works, (b)
the status a multinational businessman derives from his corporate

position and role, and (c) the nature of demands made upon the
executive by his superiors and co-workers.

2. There is a threefold impact of U.S. MNBs in the field of
East-West trade and investment policy: (a) U.S. MNBs act to lead
and sustain particular foreign policy issues, (b) U.S. MNBs provide
an independent base of information utilized by government policy
makers, and (c) U.S. MNBs are identified with interest groups
representative of the total U.S. business community.

3. U.S. MNBs and U.S. government officials employ different
policy-making and operating styles. MNBs operate on the basis of
a financial strategy. To develop profit opportunities on a case-by-
case and/or country-by-country basis, multinational executives
weigh the profits and losses of each trade and investment program.
Bureaucrats operate on the basis of national political goals. To
fulfill U.S. foreign policy objectives abroad, U.S. government
officials weigh the political risk-gain alternatives of trade and
investment policies in particular countries.

4. As institutions, U.S. multinational corporations affect
the political role behavior of their multinational businessmen.
In multinational corporations, generalized and specialized role
functions are defined. Politically active roles for corporate
executives are not explicitly defined.

5. Of the entire sample of 35 executives and bureaucrats
interviewed, 51 percent ranked highest the formal, direct role.
The formal, direct role involved frequent personal contact with
bureaucrats through written and verbal communication as well as
face-to-face executive-bureaucrat meetings. Respondents
believed this role allowed for the widest participation of U.S. MNBs
in the conduct of U.S. foreign policy on East-West trade and investment issues. When East-West policy differences arose between
MNBs and U.S. government officials, 70 percent of the executives
and 80 percent of the bureaucrats interviewed said the differences
were resolved by U.S. MNBs' reformulating their position to adapt
to U.S. government policy.

6. A negligible amount of role conflict emerged from both
groups. Only 2 of the 35 respondents believed U.S. MNBs were not
filling the role they wanted MNBs to play in the conduct of U.S.
foreign policy. The absence of role conflict derived from two
sources:

First, respondents believe that MNBs represent a source of
vast information which government policy makers find valuable in
determining East-West trade and investment policies. Second,
90 percent of the MNBs and 26 percent of the bureaucrats sampled
believed they have backgrounds similar to each other. Educational

training, past business, and prior government employment provided
experiential ties between MNBs and U. S. government officials.

This study also provided several conceptual research findings.
These are summarized as follows:

1. Since World War II, the resource-self-sufficient U. S.
economy has been transformed into an increasingly resource-
dependent economy.

2. Economics and politics have become inseparable ingredients of international affairs.

3. Trade has become a key element in the United States'
overall policy of detente with the Soviet Union.

4. Despite its deep involvement in world economic affairs
and the key roles played by U. S. business overseas, the U. S.
government remains heir to a lack of cooperation between
business and government.

5. The conflict between national governments and transnational organizations is clearly complementary rather than
duplicative.

IMPLICATIONS OF THE STUDY: POLICY ASPECTS

This study has implications for both practitioners of international business and politics and the development of a field of
study in entrepreneurial politics. This research serves to present
a body of knowledge in a subject overlooked in the literature
previously available. The leading books and articles on international business and politics have not dwelt on the problem of the
roles U. S. MNBs can play in the conduct of U. S. foreign policy
in the East-West trade and investment field. No studies in the
literature utilize role theory to explain the contribution U. S. MNBs
can make to the conduct of U. S. foreign policy. This attempt
to fill the vacuum will have some relevance to U. S. multinational
businessmen's strategies and provide an elementary theoretical
base.

The findings have implications especially for U. S. MNBs not
presently participating in the conduct of U. S. foreign policy in
the fields of East-West trade and investment. What is now certain
is that MNBs need to express their views on issues such as bulk
agricultural commodity exports or technology transfer sales to
Eastern Europe. Several respondents emphasized this point.
Although the U. S. public is aware of organized labor's impact
on U. S. foreign policy through the AFL-CIO and George Meany,
the U. S. business community has not acted to counterbalance labor's
influence. Only through adequate information-gathering and use of

mass public opinion appeals can U.S. business representatives
attain balanced public opinion response to their views.

U.S. MNBs lack a complete understanding of the direct,
formal role they can play in the conduct of U.S. foreign policy. The
collective and individual impact U.S. MNBs can have begins with
educating the American people to the contribution MNBs and their
corporations make to the welfare of the United States. Two specific
measures can be taken to expand the direct, formal role U.S. MNBs
play in the conduct of U.S. foreign policy.

First, there must be an overall international business organization which utilizes U.S. MNBs to provide legitimate, institutionalized
inputs into the U.S. foreign affairs bureaucracy. This organization
should be a Multinational Executives' Council on Foreign Relations.
The Council would select U.S. MNBs for one- to two-year periods
as International Business Fellows or IBF. The IBF would analyze
critical U.S. foreign policy questions from the multinational
executives' perspective. Operational problems involving export
licensing procedures, grain inspection programs, and market
development programs for sales of industrial products and bulk
agricultural commodities would be the subject of position papers
given directly to the president and Congress. Substantive policy
questions, such as how to eliminate constitutional bars to U.S.
investment in the Eastern European nations could be analyzed.
This organization would encourage high-level bureaucrats to
participate. By arranging one-year tours of duties for State,
Commerce, Treasury Department, and other officials with this
Multinational Executives' Council on Foreign Relations, emerging
East-West trade and investment problems could be handled by
bureaucrats and executives 12 to 18 months before the bureaucracy
tackled these problems. In this way, U.S. MNBs would make a
significant contribution to the initial formulation aspects of
foreign policy issues in the East-West field.

Second, executive-diplomat exchanges produce high mutual
returns among U.S. government participants. The work of
Chris Argyris is instructive. He studied the living system of the
Foreign Service and State Department through week-long residential
seminars with FSOs. Such seminars for executives and diplomats
require full U.S. government financial support. The State Department has already prepared a computerized list of over one thousand
corporate executives. These executives assist bureaucrats in
understanding a welter of international business problems. Moreover, executives meeting with diplomats learn about the intricacies
of bureaucratic politics and the policy-making process. Indeed,
as the U.S. government embraces resources diplomacy, U.S.
MNBs should be encouraged to become astute political actors.

The U.S. government must take the initiative in bringing together MNBs and bureaucrats with complementary attributes. Conducted through the State Department's Office of Private Cooperation and the Foreign Service Institute, widespread executive-bureaucrat training programs would focus on developing joint executive-diplomat responses to critical foreign commercial problems and policies.

IMPLICATIONS OF ENTREPRENEURIAL POLITICS AS A FIELD OF STUDY

The development of a body of literature dealing with entrepreneurial politics requires attention. It would serve as the connecting link between practitioners of international business and scholars of international politics. At present, few diplomats fully comprehend international business operations. Moreover, international business school curriculums do not emphasize the international political constraints acting upon U.S. MNBs. Specifically, there is need for a series of case studies written by former bureaucrats who are now U.S. MNBs as well as studies by U.S. MNBs who enter the government. Through comparison and contrast of their experiences as MNBs and government officials, the authors would explain how they perceived and responded to issues of U.S. commercial policy from alternative role positions.

The main contribution of these findings to the literature relates to the several different roles that U.S. MNBs can play in the conduct of U.S. foreign policy in the East-West trade and investment field. It has been shown that both U.S. MNBs and bureaucrats ranked highest the direct, formal participation of U.S. MNBs in the conduct of foreign policy. However, a number of factors prevent U.S. MNBs from assuming this role. Factors such as indifference or MNB misunderstanding the government policy maker's position need identification.

Based upon these findings, when faced with highly controversial political issues, most U.S. MNCs prefer a low-profile strategy. But the emerging issues of U.S. foreign policy are highly political ones. East-West diplomatic issues encompass Eastern European state trading systems, increasing U.S. resource scarcity, and East-West commercial interdependence. MNBs need additional training to plan for these issues. For U.S. MNBs to comprehend such political trends, U.S. MNCs must provide their MNBs with support and incentives to acquire formal or informal training in East-West relations.

In previous studies, much time has been devoted to the problems of defining a multinational corporation or the pros

and cons of MNCs' activities. The findings of this study suggest the
need to examine specific issues of mutual concern to both U. S.
MNBs and U. S. government officials. These areas would include
the following:

1. The institutionalization of executive-bureaucrat
policy planning sessions within the government. Joint executive-
bureaucrat sessions could examine issues such as promoting East-
West trade and investment; facilitating U. S. agricultural export
sales in Eastern Europe; and establishing procedural rules with
a right of appeal to U. S. MNCs transferring technology into the
Soviet bloc economies.
2. Development of a code of international corporate conduct
specifying guidelines for MNBs activities in the area of overseas
payments, the gathering and dissemination of technical information,
and the use by the government and U. S. intelligence agencies of
U. S. MNBs as unintended instruments of influence abroad.
3. Analysis of the contribution U. S. MNBs make to the
interpretation, evaluation, and implementation of U. S. foreign
policy objectives in specific programs.
4. How MNBs can utilize their international business expertise
to operationally strengthen selected U. S. foreign policy initiatives.

One aspect of the findings that tends to differ from the commonly
accepted view of the literature of international business and politics
is the limited boundaries of each of these fields of study. On the
one hand, it is generally believed that U. S. MNBs act primarily on
a profit or loss basis. Yet in international and domestic politics,
bureaucrats are generally believed to act out of concerns for
power. This study, however, has shown that neither premise
suffices.
Divergent executive-bureaucrat interpretations of government
policies will arise. In some cases, MNBs do not understand the
political decisions made by bureaucrats. Decisions a MNB would
consider unlikely because of economic losses, for political reasons
become U. S. policy. One example is the suspension of Soviet-
American grain sales. Clearly, Soviet sales have disrupted U. S.
commodity markets because of the unexpectedness and swiftness of
Soviet purchases. However, suspension of U. S. bulk agricultural export
sales to the Soviets can serve as bargaining leverage to induce
Soviet flexibility in another diplomatic area such as the SALT II
negotiations. Kissinger's linkage diplomacy can cause executives
and bureaucrats to propose alternative interpretations of government
policies.

American MNBs' global operating strategies involve their multinational corporations with numerous political relationships with diverse host governments. What is needed is a separate field of study devoted to the analysis of intergovernmental commercial and political relationships involving MNCs and their representatives. This field of study is entrepreneurial politics.

Entrepreneurial politics is the body of knowledge providing the economic-political trade-offs involved with implementing given foreign policy objectives. Entrepreneurial politics examines the policy consequences to MNCs and governments of alternative economic-political decision trade-offs. In addition, studies in entrepreneurial politics provide business-government leaders with knowledge of the political implications of U.S. MNBs' commercial activities. For example, U.S. MNBs' goal is to become competitive in the Eastern European high-technology product market. Therefore, the aim of research in the field of entrepreneurial politics focuses on matching MNBs' operating expertise with U.S. foreign policy objectives. These objectives would be designed to support specific U.S. MNBs' goals such as becoming competitive in Eastern Europe's high-technology product market. This study suggests that research focusing on MNBs' production, management, marketing, and financial expertise should be analyzed as a means of implementing U.S. East-West trade and investment policies.

DR. C. LESTER HOGAN'S RECOMMENDED REFORMS
OF THE EXPORT LICENSE CONTROL PROCESS*

1. Decision-making committees or boards of experts should
be created by the government to consider and to promulgate guidelines for the transfer of sensitive technology to Eastern European
countries. These committees should be comprised of independent,
technical personnel; they should not contain members of particular
companies interested in the results of such guidelines. Guidelines
issued by these government committees and approved by the
president or the appropriate cabinet member should represent
binding government policy.

2. Each of these committees should seek input from the
various companies in the industries affected by the guidelines to
be issued, in order to insure that industry perspectives are fully
considered. Such presentations, whenever appropriate, should be
confidential so that companies can discuss sensitive, commercial
information with these committees.

3. These guidelines should be developed in official or
semiofficial rule-making proceedings, allowing comments by
interested individuals before final promulgation. Congress
should consider subjecting the promulgation of these guidelines
to all or part of the rule-making procedures of the Administrative
Procedures Act. In addition, these guidelines should be reviewed
periodically to make certain that they reflect national security
demands as technological, commercial, and defense requirements
change.

4. Individual companies which are interested in negotiating
agreements with Eastern European countries should be afforded the

---

*From U.S. Congress, Senate, Committee on Foreign
Affairs. Multinational Corporations and United States Foreign
Policy, Hearings before the Subcommittee on Multinational
Corporations, 93rd Cong. , 2nd sess. on Investments by Multinational
Companies in the Communist Bloc Countries, June 17, 19, and July
17, 18, 19, and 22, 1974, Part 10, Washington, D.C. : Government
Printing Office, 1975, pp. 392-93.

153

opportunity, but not required, to confer privately with the appropriate committee in advance of reaching such agreements. This procedure would allow interested companies to save the expense and time of negotiating agreements which might later turn out to be unacceptable.

5. As the Office of Export Administration makes individual decisions under these guidelines, such decisions should, to a certain extent, be made public. The precedents created by such decisions, without identifying the private parties and the commercial arrangements in all of their details, could be provided in an abstract form without the mention of names or other confidential information. Through this process, a body of export license "case law" would become available to industry as particular guidelines were fleshed out by individual export license decisions. Similar sanitizing procedures before publication are now used for tax rulings and Custom Service decisions.

6. Upon denial or partial denial of an export control application by the government, the applying party should have an opportunity to appeal that decision to a special appeals board. We strongly believe that these export license questions are sufficiently significant that if a denial takes place at a lower level of the bureaucracy, the affected company should have a right, through an established mechanism, to appeal that decision and present arguments for its reversal.

7. Any system of license application review and decision making should include time limits to insure that decisions on individual application are made in a timely fashion. These standards should be similar to those contained in the pending versions of the Export Administration Act Amendments of 1974, which apply to the expanded "short supply" authority for export license denials. This type of procedural framework would save expenses for individual companies and allow them to remain "time competitive" with foreign competitors that do not face similar delays in applying for export control license approval. We believe that these types of deadlines could be met if—as we have suggested—major policy questions have been resolved in the process of formulating general guidelines.

8. In order to insure fairness to each case where a license is denied, the Office of Export Administration should be required to give reasonably detailed grounds for such a rejection to the license applicant and have an abstract of those grounds made publicly available—as previously discussed. This procedure will aid in fleshing out the general public guidelines and will insure that decision makers can provide a reasoned justification for their decision within the framework of the guidelines and existing "precedents."

TYPES OF COOPERATION ARRANGEMENTS*

Robert Starr

Coproduction and Specialization

Perhaps the most frequent forms of industrial cooperation, and also the most complex, are coproduction and specialization. Each partner may produce certain components of a final product for subsequent assembly by either partner or both; or each partner may produce certain components within a range of final products for exchange with the other partner—usually on the basis of technology supplied by one of the partners but sometimes on the basis of the partners' respective technologies or as a result of joint research and development. Such arrangements also tend to involve marketing cooperation as well, with the partners acting as agents for each other in their respective markets. The products usually carry the trademark of the selling partner, but sometimes carry a joint trademark.

Subcontracting

Under this common form of cooperation, the Eastern enterprise typically produces in accordance with designs and specifications supplied by its western partner (sometimes machinery and equipment and parts are also supplied) and delivers an agreed-upon quantity of finished or semifinished goods or spare parts. Such arrangements may be for a short period of time, merely to supplement the capacity of the Western partner; more frequently, they entail long-term relationships between the parties.

---

* From "Evolving Patterns of East-West Business Transactions: An Introductory Note on Cooperation Agreements," in East-West Business Transactions, pp. 490-92. Edited by Robert Starr. (New York: Praeger, 1974).

Cooperation Involving Licensing

The bare license of the right to exploit industrial property rights does not in itself constitute a cooperation arrangement. However, licensing agreements can involve cooperation, as when payment is to be made in products or components related to or resulting from a licensing arrangement accompanied by the supply of machinery, equipment and/or technical assistance, and sometimes component parts.

Supply of Complete Plant or Production Lines

This type of cooperation involves the sale of a complete plant or production line with at least partial payment in resulting product; frequently the Western partner also supplies drawings, equipment, and know-how, trains the buyer's personnel, and assists in the start-up and operation of the Eastern plant.

Joint Ventures

The most common form of joint venture involves marketing of products made in Eastern countries through a jointly owned enterprise established in a Western country, with both partners contributing capital and sharing in management decisions as well as profits and losses. In some cases these enterprises are also concerned with assembly of products supplied by the Eastern partner, and not infrequently they are involved in two-way trade as well.

Investment joint ventures are now permitted in Yugoslavia and in two Comecon countries, Romania and Hungary, under legal provisions specially enacted for this purpose. In Yugoslavia, Romania, and Hungary it is now possible to establish joint ventures within their territories that have legal characteristics similar to joint ventures in market-economy countries—with comanagement, coownership of capital, and sharing of profits and risks—to undertake production, marketing and other operations.

Joint Tendering and Other Joint Projects

Examples of cooperation in joint tendering for work projects in either country, or more frequently in a third country (often a developing country), are numerous. Usually one of the partners acts as the main contractor—depending upon a variety of political,

financial, and other factors. The Eastern partner normally acts as
the main contractor on a project in another East European country.

Research and Development

Cooperation in research and development generally involves
the exchange of information on research and development activities
by the partners, frequently with exchanges of inspection missions,
joint conferences, and even the establishment of joint committees
to examine common problems. More intensive cooperation in this
field may reinvolve joint research and development projects, often
with respect to equipment produced by each of the partners.

Other Forms of Cooperation

This brief listing of categories is intended only to illustrate
in broad outline the main forms of East-West cooperation; it is
by no means complete. Indeed, one of the most fascinating aspects
of East-West trade is the challenge posed by the need to devise new
legal patterns to meet perceived needs. Frequently, a cooperation
arrangement may involve a combination of elements, such as the
sale of machinery and equipment, licensing of know-how, and the
repurchase of product by the Western partner. Within any listing of
categories of East-West cooperation, it would also be necessary
to include contracts that have been identified as cooperation agreements under intergovernmental agreements and/or pursuant to
applicable law in a particular country.

BIBLIOGRAPHY

BOOKS

Aitken, Thomas. The Multinational Man: The Role of the Manager Abroad. New York: John Wiley and Sons, 1973.

Barnet, Richard J., and Müller, Ronald E. Global Reach: The Power of the Multinational Corporations. New York: Simon and Schuster, 1975.

Behrman, Jack N. Conflicting Constraints on the Multinational Enterprise: Potential for Resolution. New York: Council of the Americas and Fund for Multinational Management Education, 1974.

_____. International Business-Government Communications: H. S. Structures, Actors and Issues. Lexington, Mass: D. C. Heath, 1975.

_____. National Interests and the Multinational Enterprise: Tensions Among the North Atlantic Countries. Englewood Cliffs, N. J.: Prentice-Hall, Inc., 1970.

_____. Some Patterns in the Rise of the Multinational Enterprise. Chapel Hill, N. C.: Graduate School of Business Administration, 1969.

_____. U. S. International Business and Governments. New York: McGraw Hill, 1971.

Bell, Daniel. The Coming of the Post-Industrial Society: A Venture in Social Forecasting. New York: Basic Books, Inc., Publishers, 1973.

Blake, David H., ed. The Multinational Corporation. The Annals of the American Academy of Political and Social Science, September 1972.

Bonner, Hubert. Group Dynamics: Principles and Applications. New York: The Ronald Press Company, 1959.

Brooke, Michael Z. , and Remmers, H. Lee. The Multinational
    Company in Europe. London: Longman Group Limited, 1972.

____. The Strategy of Multinational Enterprise. London: Longman
    Group Limited, 1972.

Brookstone, Jeffrey M. "Entrepreneurial Politics: The Role of
    American Multinational Businessmen in the Conduct of U. S.
    Foreign Policy; A Case Study of East-West Trade and Invest-
    ment Policies. " Ph. D. dissertation (on which this study is
    based), George Washington University, 1976, pp. i-408.

Chorafas, Dimitris N. Developing the International Executive. New
    York: American Management Association, Inc. , 1967.

Cracco, Etienne Francis. The Nature and Perception of Political
    Risk for the International Corporation: An Exploratory Analysis
    with Special Reference to Brazil. Ann Arbor, Michigan: Uni-
    versity Microfilms, 72-29, 947, 1972.

Drucker, Peter F. Management. New York: Harper & Row, 1974.

____. Men, Ideas and Politics. New York: Harper & Row, 1971.

____. Technology, Management and Society. New York: Harper & Row,
    1970.

____. The Age of Discontinuity. New York: Harper & Row, 1969.

____. The Effective Executive. New York: Harper & Row, 1967.

Eells, Richard. Global Corporations: The Emerging System of
    World Economic Power. New York: Interbook, Inc. , 1972.

Giffen, James Henry. The Legal and Practical Aspects of Trade with
    the Soviet Union. New York: Praeger, 1971.

Grub, Phillip D. American-East European Trade. Washington, D. C. :
    National Press, 1969.

Harr, John E. The Professional Diplomat. Princeton: Princeton
    University Press, 1969.

Hodgson, Richard C. ; Levinson, Daniel J. ; and Zaleznik, Abraham.
    The Executive Role Constellation: An Analysis of Personality

and Role Relations in Management. Boston: Harvard University Press, 1965.

Jacoby, Neil. Multinational Oil: A Study in Industrial Dynamics. New York: Macmillan Co. , 1974.

Kalb, Marvin, and Kalb, Bernard. Kissinger. Boston: Little, Brown and Company, 1974.

Kapoor, Ashok. Planning for International Business Negotiation. Cambridge, Mass. : Ballinger Publishing Co. , 1975.

Kapoor, A. , and Grub, Phillip D. , eds. The Multinational Enterprise in Transition. Princeton: Darwin Press, 1972.

Kindleberger, Charles P. Power and Money: The Economics of International Politics and the Politics of International Economics. New York: Basic Books, Inc. , 1970.

Krech, David, and Crutchfield, Richard S. Elements of Psychology. New York: Alfred A. Knopf, 1959.

____. Theory and Problems of Social Psychology. New York: McGraw-Hill, 1948.

Kretschmar, Jr. , Robert S. , and Foor, Robin. The Potential for Joint Ventures in Eastern Europe. New York: Praeger, 1972.

Levinson, Harry. The Exceptional Executive: A Psychological Conception. Cambridge: Harvard University Press, 1968.

Marchetti, Victor, and Marks, John D. The CIA and the Cult of Intelligence. New York: Alfred A. Knopf, Inc. , 1974.

Miller, Robert W. The Creative Interface: International Business-Government Relations. Washington, D. C. : The American University, 1970.

Nehrt, Lee C. ; Truitt, J. Frederick; and Wright, Richard W. International Business Research: Past, Present, and Future. Bloomington, Ind. : Graduate School of Business, Indiana University, 1970.

Payne, Stanley L. The Art of Asking Questions. Princeton: Princeton University Press, 1951.

Pisar, Samuel. Coexistence and Commerce. New York: McGraw-Hill, 1970.

Robinson, Richard D. International Management. New York: Holt, Rinehart and Winston, Inc., 1967.

Robock, Stefan H., and Simmonds, Kenneth. International Business and Multinational Enterprises. Homewood, Ill.: Richard D. Irwin, Inc., 1973.

Said, Abdul A., and Simmons, Luiz R., eds. The New Sovereigns: Multinational Corporations as World Powers. Englewood Cliffs, N.J.: Prentice-Hall, Inc., 1975.

Sampson, Anthony. The Sovereign State of ITT. New York: Stein and Day Incorporated, 1973.

Schurmann, Franz. The Logic of World Power: An Inquiry into the Origins, Currents, and Contradictions of World Politics. New York: Pantheon Books, 1974.

Skolnikoff, Eugene B. Science, Technology and American Foreign Policy. Cambridge: M. I. T. Press, 1967.

Spanier, John. American Foreign Policy Since World War II. New York: Praeger, 1973.

Tugendhat, Christopher. The Multinationals. New York: Random House, 1972.

Vernon, Raymond. Sovereignty at Bay: The Multinational Spread of U.S. Enterprises. New York: Basic Books, Inc., 1971.

Wilczynski, Jozef. The Economics and Politics of East-West Trade. New York: Praeger, 1969.

Wilensky, Harold L. Organizational Intelligence: Knowledge and Policy in Government and Industry. New York: Basic Books, Inc., 1967.

Wilkens, Mira. The Emergence of Multinational Enterprise: American Business Abroad from the Colonial Era to 1914. Cambridge: Harvard University Press, 1970.

Wilkens, Mira. The Maturing of Multinational Enterprise. Cambridge: Harvard University Press, 1974.

Zeisal, Hans. Say It With Figures. New York: Harper & Row, 1968.

ARTICLES

Aharoni, Yair. "On the Definition of a Multinational Corporation." In The Multinational Enterprise in Transition, pp. 17-18. Edited by A. Kapoor and Phillip D. Grub. Princeton, N.J.: Darwin Press, 1972.

Alger, Chadwick F. "The Multinational Corporation and the Future International System." In The Multinational Corporation, pp. 104-15. Edited by David H. Black. The Annals of the American Academy of Political and Social Science 402, September, 1972.

Argyris, Chris. "The CEO's Behavior: Key to Organizational Development." Harvard Business Review 51, no. 2 (March-April 1973): 55-64.

Bacchus, William I. "Diplomacy for the 70's: An Afterview and Appraisal." American Political Science Review 68, no. 2 (June 1974): 736-48.

Ball, George W. "Cosmocorp: The Importance of Being Stateless." in World Business: Promise and Problems, pp. 330-38. Edited by Courtney C. Brown. New York: Macmillan, 1970.

Behrman, Jack N. "Actors and Factors in Policy Decisions on Foreign Direct Investment." World Development 2, no. 8 (August 1974): 1-14.

____. "Multinational Corporations and National Sovereignty." In World Business: Promise and Problems, pp. 114-25. Edited by Courtney C. Brown. New York: Macmillan, 1970.

Benoit, Emile. "Interdependence on a Small Planet." In World Business: Promise and Problems, pp. 13-28. Edited by Courtney C. Brown. New York: Macmillan, 1970.

Blount, Winton M. "The Businessman in Government." The Conference Board Record 11, no. 2 (February 1974): 36-37.

Boddewyn, J. "External Affairs at Four Levels in U.S. Multinationals." Industrial Relations 12, no. 2 (May 1973): 239-47.

Boddweyn, J., and Kapoor, Ashok. "The External Relations of American Multinational Enterprises." International Studies Quarterly 16, no. 4 (December 1972): 433-53.

Bradley, Gene E., and Bursk, Edward C. "Multinationalism and the 29th Day." Harvard Business Review 50, no. 1 (January-February, 1972): 37-47.

Brzezinski, Zbigniew. "U.S. Foreign Policy: The Search for Focus." Foreign Affairs 51, no. 4 (July 1973): 708-27

"Businessman to Play Key Role in Advising U.S. Negotiators at Coming World Trade Talks." Commerce Today 5, no. 7 (January 6, 1975): 19-21.

Domhoff, G. William. "Playgrounds of the Powerful: How Fat Cats Keep in Touch." Psychology Today 9, no. 3 (August 1975): 44-48.

Eells, Richard. "Do Multinational Corporations Stand Guilty as Charged?" Business and Society Review 11 (Autumn 1974): 81-87.

_____. "Multinational Corporations: The Intelligence Function." In World Business: Promise and Problems, pp. 140-55. Edited by Courtney C. Brown. New York: Macmillan, 1970.

Falk, Richard, and Maynes, Jr., Charles W. "Who Pays for Foreign Policy? Comments." Foreign Policy, no. 18 (Spring 1975): 92-122.

Galnoor, Itzhak. "Government Secrecy: Exchanges, Intermediaries, and Middlemen." Public Administration Review 35, no. 1 (January-February, 1975): 32-41.

Garnham, David. "Foreign Service Elitism and U.S. Foreign Affairs." Public Administration Review 35, no. 1 (January-February, 1975): 44-51.

_____. "State Department Rigidity: Testing a Psychological Hypothesis." International Studies Quarterly 18, no. 1 (March 1974): 31-39.

Grossman, Gregory. "Prospects for U. S. -Soviet Trade." American Economic Review 64, no. 2 (May 1974): 289-93.

Grzybowski, Kazimerz. "Comecon." In East-West Business Transactions, pp. 117-36. Edited by Robert Starr. New York: Praeger, 1974.

Haider, Michael L. "Tomorrow's Executive: A Man for All Countries." Columbia Journal of World Business 1, no. 1 (Winter 1966): 107-13.

Havighorst, Carl R. "U. S. Super-Corporations in Food: FE Analyzes the Top 75." Food Engineering no. 1 (January 1975): 45-55.

Heilbroner, Robert L. "The Clouded Crystal Ball." American Economic Review 64, no. 2 (May 1974): 121-24.

Henderson, Richard Ivan. "The Best of Two Worlds: The Entrepreneurial Manager." Journal of Small Business Management 12, no. 4 (October 1974): 1-2.

Hume, David L. "Foreign Market Development—A Government/ Industry Team." Foreign Agriculture 13, no. 21 (May 26, 1975): 3-5.

Huntington, Samuel P. "Transnational Organizations in World Politics." World Politics 25, no. 3 (April 1973): 333-68.

Johnson, Michael J. , and Bradley, Gene E. "A New Partnership— Businessmen and Diplomats—They're Working Toward the Same Goals." Nations Business 62, no. 9 (September 1974): 74-80.

Katz, Daniel. "Field Studies." In Research Methods in the Behavioral Sciences, pp. 56-97. Edited by Leon Festinger and Daniel Katz. New York: Holt, Rinehart and Winston, 1953.

Keegan, Warren J. "Multinational Scanning: A Study of the Information Sources Utilized by Headquarters Executives in Multinational Companies." Administrative Science Quarterly 19, no. 3 (September 1974): 411-21.

Kendall, Donald M. "The Need for Multinationals." Columbia Journal of World Business 8, no. 3 (Fall 1973): 103-06.

Keohane, Robert O. , and Nye, Jr. , Joseph S. "Transnational Rela-
    tions and World Politics." International Organization 25, no. 3
    (Summer 1971): 329-58

Kennan, George F. "After the Cold War. American Foreign Policy
    in the 1970s." Foreign Affairs 51, no. 1 (October 1972): 210-
    27.

Kindl, Herbert J. "The Professional Generalist Manager." Defense
    Management Journal 11, no. 1 (January 1975): 54-62.

Kindleberger, Charles P. "The Multinational Corporation in a World
    of Militant Developing Countries." In Global Companies: The
    Political Economy of World Business, pp. 70-84. Edited by
    George W. Ball. Englewood Cliffs, N. J. : Prentice-Hall, 1975.

"Kissinger on Oil, Food, and Trade." Business Week, no. 2363
    (January 13, 1975): 66-76.

Maisonrouge, Jacques G. "How a Multinational Corporation Appears
    to Its Managers." In Global Companies: The Political Economy
    of World Business, pp. 11-20. Edited by George W. Ball.
    Englewood Cliffs, N. J. : Prentice-Hall, 1975.

Malek, Frederic V. "Mr. Executive Goes to Washington." Harvard
    Business Review 50, no. 5 (September-October, 1972): 63-68.

Modelski, George. "Multinational Business: A Global Perspective."
    International Studies Quarterly 16, no. 4 (December 1972):
    407-32.

Nye, Joseph S. , Jr. "Multinational Corporations in World Politics."
    Foreign Affairs 53, no. 1 (October 1974): 153-75.

____, and Rubin, Seymour J. "The Long Range Political Role of the
    Multinational Corporation." In Global Companies: The Political
    Economy of World Business, pp. 126-134. Edited by George W.
    Ball. Englewood Cliffs, N. J. : Prentice-Hall, 1975.

Perlmutter, Howard V. "A View of the Future." In The New Sov-
    ereigns: Multinational Corporations as World Powers, pp. 167-
    86. Edited by Abdul A. Said and Luiz R. Simmons. Engle-
    wood Cliffs, N. J. : Prentice Hall, 1975.

Perlmutter, Howard V. "The Tortuous Evolution of the Multinational Corporation." In The Multinational Enterprise in Transition, pp. 53-66. Edited by A. Kapoor and Phillip D. Grub. Princeton: Darwin Press, 1972.

Phillips, Warren R. "Where Have All the Theories Gone?" World Politics 26, no. 2 (January 1974): 155-88.

Powell, Reed M. , and Hostiuck, K. Tim. "The Business Executive's Role in Politics." Business Horizons 15, no. 4 (August 1972): 49-56.

Ray, Dennis M. "Corporations and American Foreign Relations." In The Multinational Corporation, pp. 80-92. Edited by David W. Black. The Annals of the American Academy of Political and Social Science 403, September 1972.

Reichley, A. James. "A Foreign Policy for the Era of Interdependence." Fortune 91, no. 4 (April 1975): 153-60.

Russell, Francis H. "Formulating Foreign Policy." Orbis 17, no. 4 (Winter 1974): 1344-53.

Russett, Bruce M. , and Hanson, Betty C. "How Corporate Executives See America's Role in the World." Fortune 89, no. 5 (May 1974): 165-68.

Shershnev, E. S. "Soviet-American Economic Relations at the New Stage." Soviet and Eastern European Foreign Trade 11, no. 1 (Spring 1975): 57-75.

Shetty, Y. K. "International Manager: A Role Profile." Management International Review 11, no. 4-5 (1971): 19-25.

Skolnikoff, Eugene B. "Science and Technology: The Implications for International Institutions." International Organization 25 (Fall 1971): 759-75.

Sorensen, Theodore C. "Watergate and American Foreign Policy." The World Today 30, no. 12 (December 1974): 497-503.

Starr, Robert. "Evolving Patterns of East-West Business Transactions: Introductory Note on Cooperation Agreements." In East-West Business Transactions, pp. 488-98. Edited by Robert Starr. New York: Praeger, 1974.

Starr, Robert. "Introductory Note on Contracting with Enterprises in State-Planned Economies." In East-West Business Transactions, pp. 449-61. Edited by Robert Starr. New York: Praeger, 1974.

Stolte, Darwin. "Team Effort Boosts U. S. Farm Exports." Foreign Agriculture 13, no. 21 (May 26, 1975): 7-11, 30.

"The Impact of Multinational Corporations on the Development Process and on International Relations: The Report of the Group of Eminent Persons to Study the Role of Multinational Corporations on Development and on International Relations." International Legal Materials 13, no. 4 (July 1974): 800-69.

"Top 500 DOD Research and Development Contractors." Aviation Week and Space Technology 102, no. 5 (February 3, 1975): 50-55.

Uttal, Bro. "The Fortune Directory of the 500 Largest Industrial Corporations." Fortune 91, no. 5 (May 1975): 208-35.

Vagts, Detlev F. "The Multinational Enterprise: A New Challenge for Transnational Law." Harvard Law Review 83, no. 4 (February 1970): 739-92.

Venu, S. "The Multinationals and Developing Societies: Profile of the Future." Futures 6, no. 2 (April 1974): 133-41.

Vernon, Raymond. "Competition Policy Toward Multinational Corporations." American Economic Review 64, no. 2 (May 1974): 276-82.

____. "Does Society Also Profit?" Foreign Policy, no. 13 (Winter 1973-74): 103-18.

____. "Multinational Business and National Goals." International Organization 25 (Summer 1971): 693-705.

____; Barnet, Richard J.; and Müller, Ronald E. "An Exchange on Multinationals." Foreign Policy, no. 5 (Summer 1974): 83-92.

Vesper, Karl H. "Entrepreneurship, A Fast Emerging Area in Management Studies." Journal of Small Business Management 12, no. 14 (October 1974): 8-15.

Wilkens, Mira. "The Businessman Abroad." In The American Business Executive, pp. 83-94. The Annals of the American Academy of Political and Social Science 368, November 1966.

PUBLIC DOCUMENTS

Casey, William J. "Prospects and Policy on East-West Trade." Department of State Bulletin 68 (May 21, 1973): 638-43.

Hartman, Arthur A. "U. S.-Soviet Detente: Perceptions and Purposes." Department of State Bulletin 70 (June 3, 1974): 597-602.

Ingersoll, Robert S. "The Global Economy." Address by the deputy secretary of state before the Economic Club of Detroit, Cobo Hall, Detroit, Michigan, February 18, 1975. Washington, D. C.: Department of State Press release no. 74.

Johnson, U. Alexis. "Complexities and Accomplishments of U. S. Foreign Policy." Department of State Bulletin 70 (June 10, 1974): 633-35.

Kissinger, Henry A. "A Just Consensus, A Stable Order, A Durable Peace." Department of State Bulletin 69 (October 15, 1973): 469-73.

____. "An Age of Interdependence: Common Disaster or Community." Department of State Bulletin 71, no. 1842 (October 14, 1974): 498-504.

____. "Detente with the Soviet Union: The Reality of Competition and the Imperative of Cooperation." Department of State Bulletin 71, no. 1842 (October 14, 1974): 505-19.

____. "U. S. Foreign Policy: Finding Strength Through Adversity." Washington, D. C.: Department of State, Bureau of Public Affairs, Office of Media Services, April 17, 1975, press release no. 204.

Murphy, Robert D. Commission on the Organization of the Government for the Conduct of Foreign Policy. Washington, D. C.: Government Printing Office, June 1975.

Martin, Edwin M. "International Cooperation in Feeding the World's Hungry." Department of State 70 (June 10, 1974): 621-26.

Schoonover, David M. "The Soviet Feed-Livestock Economy: Prelim-
    inary Findings on Performance and Trade Implications." In
    Prospects for Agricultural Trade with the USSR, pp. 24-42.
    U. S. Department of Agriculture, the Foreign Demand and
    Competition Division, Economic Research Service, Joseph W.
    Willett, Director. ERS-Foreign 356. Washington, D. C. :
    Government Printing Office, April 1974.

Sisco, Joseph J. "America's Foreign Policy Agenda: Toward the
    Year 2000." Department of State Bulletin 72, no. 1859
    (February 10, 1975): 182-87.

_____. "The U. S. Contribution to a Peaceful World Structure." Depart-
    ment of State Bulletin 70 (April 15, 1974): 381-85.

United Nations. Economic and Social Council. Commission on Trans-
    national Corporations. Draft Programme of Work on the Full
    Range of Issues Relating to Transnational Corporations. Report
    of the Secretary General. (No. E/C .10/2), March 17-28,
    1975, pp. 42-44.

United Nations. Office of Public Information. "Transnational Corpo-
    rations: Commission Gives Priority to Preparation on Conduct
    Code." UN Chronicle 12, no. 4 (April 1975): 31-32.

U. S. General Accounting Office. Export of U. S. -Manufactured
    Aircraft—Financing and Competitiveness. Washington, D. C. :
    Government Printing Office, No. B-114823, March 12, 1975.

_____. Exporters' Profits on Sales of U. S. Wheat to Russia. Washing-
    ton, D. C. : Government Printing Office, No. B-176943.

U. S. Congress. House. Committee on Foreign Affairs. Detente.
    Hearing before the Subcommittee on Europe, 93rd Cong. , 2nd
    sess. Washington, D. C. : Government Printing Office, 1974.

_____. Detente: Prospects for Increased Trade with Warsaw Pact
    Countries. Report of a Special Study Mission to the Soviet
    Union and Eastern Europe, August 22 to September 8, 1974.
    Washington, D. C. : Government Printing Office, 1974.

_____. Global Scarcities in an Interdependent World. Hearings before
    the Subcommittee on Foreign Economic Policy, 93rd Cong. ,
    2nd sess. Washington, D. C. : Government Printing Office,
    1974.

U. S. Congress. House. International Relations Committee. Chronol-
ogies of Major Developments in Selected Areas of International
Relations, 94th Cong. , 1st sess. Washington, D. C. : Government Printing Office, 1975.

____. Senate. Committee on Finance. Implications of Multinational
Firms for World Trade and Investment and for U. S. Trade and
Labor. U. S. Tariff Commission Report, 93rd Cong. , 1st sess.
Washington, D. C. : Government Printing Office, 1973.

____. Subcommittee on International Trade. The Multinational Corpo-
ration and the World Economy. Committee report, 93rd Cong. ,
1st sess. Washington, D. C. : Government Printing Office,
1973.

____. Committee on Foreign Affairs. Multinational Corporations and
United States Foreign Policy, Hearings before the Subcommittee
on Multinational Corporations, 93rd Cong. , 2nd sess. on
Investments by Multinational Companies in the Communist Bloc
Countries, June 17, 19, and July 17, 18, 19, and 22, 1974,
Part 10. Washington, D. C. : Government Printing Office, 1975.

____. Subcommittee on Multinational Corporations. Western Invest-
ment in Communist Economies: A Selected Survey on Economic
Interdependence, by John P. Hardt, George D. Holliday and
Young C. Kim. Committee print, 93rd Cong. , 2nd sess.
Washington, D. C. : Government Printing Office, August 5, 1974.

U. S. Congress. Senate. Committee on Foreign Relations. U. S.
Trade and Investment in the Soviet Union and Eastern Europe:
The Role of Multinational Corporations. Committee print,
93rd Cong. , 2nd sess. Washington, D. C. : Government Printing
Office, 1974.

____. Committee on Labor and Public Welfare. The Multinational
Corporation and the National Interest. Report by Professor
Robert Gilpin, Princeton University. 93rd Cong. , 1st sess.
Washington, D. C. : Government Printing Office, 1973.

U. S. Department of Agriculture. Foreign Agricultural Service. The
Agricultural Situation in Eastern Europe, Review of 1974 and
Outlook for 1975, by the European Area, Foreign Demand and
Competition Division, Economic Research Service. Foreign
Agricultural Economic Report no. 102. Washington, D. C. :
Government Printing Office, April 1975.

U. S. Department of Agriculture. Trading With the USSR and Eastern Europe, by the Foreign Market Development and Evaluation Division. FAS M-264. Washington, D. C.: Government Printing Office, June 1975.

U. S. Department of Commerce. Domestic and International Business Administration. Bureau of East-West Trade. Export Administration Report, Fourth Quarter 1974, 110th Report on U. S. Export Controls to the President and the Congress. Washington, D. C.: Government Printing Office, 1975.

REPORTS

Chamber of Commerce of the United States. The Climate for Investment Abroad. Washington, D. C.: Chamber of Commerce, September 1974, pp. 46-50.

Griffith, William E., and Rostow, Walt W. East-West Relations: Is Detente Possible? Washington, D. C.: American Enterprise Institute for Public Policy Research, 1969.

Kendall, Donald M. The Multinational Corporation: American Mainstay in the World Economy. New York: Emergency Committee for American Trade, August 1973.

Lovell, Enid Baird. The Changing Role of the International Executive. New York: National Industrial Conference Board, Inc., Business Policy Study no. 119, 1966.

Rolfe, Sidney. The Multinational Corporation. New York: Foreign Policy Association, Inc., Headline Series no. 199, 1970.

Romanian-U. S. Economic Council, U. S. Section, Chamber of Commerce of the United States. Romanian-U. S. Joint Ventures: Background for Implementation. Washington, D. C.: Chamber of Commerce, November 1974, pp. 1-64.

NEWSPAPERS

Church, Frank. "Profits of Doom." The Washington Post, Book World, January 19, 1975, sec. F, pp. 1, 4.

"Eaton Says the C. I. A. Asked Him to Be A Spy." The New York Times, June 16, 1975, p. 38.

Finn, David. "The Business of Businessmen Is Not Just Business." The New York Times, June 28, 1975, p. 27.

Geneen, Harold. "Feed the People." The New York Times, June 16, 1975, p. 27.

Goldman, Marshall I. "The Russians Are Buying." The New York Times, July 31, 1975, p. 27.

Jensen, Michael C. "U. S. Company Payoffs Way of Life Overseas." The New York Times, May 5, 1975, pp. 1, 52.

"Prices of Commodity Future." The New York Times, August 12, 1975, p. 44.

Robbins, William. "Butz to Propose Grain Trade Plan." The New York Times, July 1, 1975, p. 18.

"Treasury Official Quits, Cites His Money Woes." The New York Times, June 19, 1975, p. 49.

abuses, grain export trade, 97

academician, as intermediary, 134

acquaintanceship ties, 138

Aerospace Industries Association, 58

AFL-CIO, 2, 148

agencies making foreign policy, 42

agribusinessmen, 140

agricultural commodities, U.S. exports of, 92, 93

Agricultural Trade Development and Assistance Act, 1954, 99

Aharoni, Yair, 3

Air America, 72-73

Alger, Chadwick F., 61, 62

American Economic Association, 139

American Enterprise Institute, 133

American Jewish Committee, 57

Anderson, Jack, 141

Argyris, Chris, 149

Armstrong, Willis C., 149

assumptions, 3

Atlantic Council, 132-33

attitude: ethnocentric, 8; geocentric, 8; polycentric, 8

background similarity, factors promoting, 138

Ball, George W., 9

bargaining, 126

basic roles, U.S. business, 16

Bechtel Corporation, 129

Behrman, Jack N., 63, 69

Bell, Daniel, 120

Bennett, Jack F., 129

Berlin Airlift, 43

Boeing Aircraft, 48, 126

Bohemian Club, 138

Bonner, Hubert, 21, 22

Bowden, Lewis, 47, 56

Bradley, Gene E., 15

Brezhnev, Leonid, 46

Brzezinski, Zbigniew, 64, 101, 111, 113

Brooke, Michael Z., 12

Brookings Institution, 133

buffer reserve, U.S. farmer as, 91

bulk commodity export sales, 94

bureaucracy, U. S. , 102

Bureaucrats and education, 37; and job responsibility, 37; and present job experience, 36; by age group, 36; by GS rating, 37; contact with U. S. MNCs, 125; receptivity to intermediaries, 132; sampled, 31; supergrade ranks, 120; type of contacts, 122

Burke-Hartke Bill, 3

business advisory groups, 70

business criticism, 120

business executive's role in politics, 23

business-government cooperation, 148

businessmen-diplomats interdependence, 15

Butz, Earl L. , 94

Ceausescu, Nicolae, 111

channels of U. S. MNB's influence, 5

chief executive officer, 1

Chorafas, Dimitris N. , 21,24

Chrisler, Donald, 90

Church, Frank, 104

CIA, 72-73

civil aviation protocol agreements, 48

clandestine activities, 2

Comecon, 46; export licenses, 104

Commission for the Reorganization of the Government in the Conduct of Foreign Policy, 64

commodity control list, 102

commodity trading, U. S. -Eastern bloc, 88

comparative matrix model, 27

competitive coexistence, 43

conceptual research findings, 148

Congress and foreign policy, 43

contacts, U. S. government officials' with U. S. MNBs, 124

containment, 43

Continental Grain, 89

contribution, former bureaucrats by U. S. MNBs, 130

Cook Industries, 89

cooperative economic relations, 46

cooperative relationships between MNBs and government officials, 59

cooperation agreements, types of, 155-57

cooperation, other forms of, 157

cooperator groups, examples of, 100

corporate political activity, 26, 147

corporate political behavior, variables, 84

corporate roles, 1

corporations, transideological, 113

criteria defining MNC, 8

cross-functional decision
making, 82-83

cultural diversity, 5

curriculum, international
business school, 150

Czechoslovakia, U.S. investment in, 53

decision making committees, 153

democratic political style, 11

detente, meaning of, 43; multiple levels of, 44; politics
of, 111-12

direct, formal MNB participation in East-West trade
and investment issues, 122;
in U.S. foreign policy, 150

direct, informal role, 143

direct role, 1

Domhoff, G. William, 138

Drucker, Peter F., 9, 77

Dubcek, Alexander, 110

Eastern European commodity
export markets, 90; exports
and imports, 45; export
licensing problems, 101;
market size, 56; semicon-
ductor market, 104-05

East-West investment, 48; MNB
influencing of, 135

East-West issues, 151; politics,
46; role for MNB, 84

East-West trade and investment
issues, informal, indirect
participation of U.S. MNB
in, 141

East-West trade policies, implementing changes in, 128

East-West Trade Policy Committee,
48

East-West trade, U.S. government
policy coordination, 48, 49

Eaton, Cyrus, 2

Economic Club of Detroit, 68

economic detente, 47; U.S. opposition to, 56; U.S.
supporters of, 56

economic management, advantages
of national system, 41

economy, resource dependent, 148

EEC, 46

Eells, Richard, 9, 68-69

Emergency Committee for American
Trade (ECAT), 12, 57

entrepreneur, function and role
of, 13

entrepreneurial politics, 14, 148;
as field of study, 150;
defined, 152

Equal Export Opportunity Act, 1972,
102

executive/bureaucrat cooperation,
98, 147; policy planning, 151

executives, defined, 77

executive/diplomat consultations, 74;
exchanges, 131, 149;

relationships, 88; seminars, 139; training programs, 150

explanatory effectiveness, 7

exploratory study, 27, 38

Export Administration Act, 1969, 102

export controls, administrative structure of, 103

exporters, defined, 3

export license, case law, 154; cost of obtaining, 109

export licensing control process, 153-54

export licensing policy, groups used to effect policy changes, 133; guidelines and precedents, 154; problems, 101, 108-09; special appeals board, 154

external relations strategy, low profile, 143

factors, research, 146

Fairchild Camera and Instrument Corporation, 104

Fairchild-Unitra case, 106-08

Falk, Richard, 10

feed grain, U.S. exports, 90

findings, research, 146-48

Finn, David, 120

firm's multinationality, 8

food corporations, 27, 28

Ford, Gerald K., 70

foreign affairs policy making, 42

Foreign Agricultural Service, 98

foreign policy, defined, 10-11

foreign service elitism, 75, 77; officers, 138; psychological flexibility, 76-77

formal, direct role, 5, 27-31, 147

formal, indirect role, 5, 27-31

Fowler, Henry H., 133

FSO Corps, 75

future Soviet-U.S. commercial relations, 57

Garnham, David, 75-76

Geneen, Harold, 1, 88

generalized tariff preferences, 17

geopolitics, Eastern Europe, 110-11

Gierek, Edward, 110

global cooperation, 42

global management approach, 79-80

global nutrition leadership, 89

global profit maximizing strategy, 1

Goldman, Marshall I., 91, 94

government business cooperation, 69-70

government functions, business effects, 69

government industry cooperator programs, 99

government officials, formerly employed by MNCs, 129

grain and wheat balances, Soviet projections, 95

grain inspection proposals, 94, 97

grain trading companies, U.S., 89

guidelines, decisions for, 153-54

Hammer, Armand, 53, 140

Hardin, Clifford, 140

Hardt, John P., 111, 114

Harr, John, 75

Henderson, Richard I., 13

hidden government, 109

high-technology sales, 122

Hogan, C. Lester, 56, 107-10, 116

host country, 5

Hostiuck, K. Tim, 23-24, 26

Hughes Aircraft, 32

Hungary, U.S. investment in, 54

Huntington, Samuel P., 67

Husak, Gustav, 110

hypothesis, psychological, 76; systemic, 76; testing, 30

IBM, global company example, 62; global contribution, 62-63; global management, 79

Ikard, Frank, 15

impact of MNB on East-West trade and investment, 57-59

implications of the study, 148

importers, defined, 4

industrial cooperation agreements, kinds of, 114, 116

industrial corporations, 27-30

industrial property rights, 73

Industry Policy Advisory Committee, IPAC, 70-71

Industry Sector Advisory Committee, ISAC, 70-71

informal, direct participation, MNBs in East-West trade and investment issues, 138

informal, direct role, 5, 28-30, 143

informal, direct ties, MNB's participation in East-West trade policies, 140

informal, indirect role, 5, 28-30, 143

Ingersoll, Robert S., 68

intelligence gathering and dissemination, 72

Interagency Operating Committee, 104

interdependence, causative factors, 42; nation-state, 40

intergovernmental units, 35

intermediaries, used in direct, informal participation, 132; use of, 135

international affairs, 147

international business organization, 149

International Business Fellows, 149

international corporate conduct, code of, 151

International Management Association, 15

international political system, changes in, 61

interviewing and data collection, 38

interviews, drawbacks and procedural safeguards, 38

intraenterprise transactions, 2

issues, East-West trade and investment, 88

ITT, 1, 88

Jackson, Henry, 47

Jackson-Vanik Amendment, 2, 47, 48, 57, 114

Johnson, Michael J. , 15

Johnson, U. Alexis, 16

joint commissions, 46

Joint Commerce-Special Trade Representative for Trade Negotiations Program, 70

joint tendering, 156

joint venture cooperative agreements, 140

joint ventures, 156

Kadar, Janos, 111

Kama Automotive Plant, 114

Katz, Daniel, 27

Kendall, Donald M. , 12, 56, 57, 134

Kennan, George F. , 40-41

Khrushchev, Nikita, 43

Kindl, Herbert J. , 82

Kissinger, Henry A. , 40, 43, 75, 144, 151

Kraft, Joseph, 141

leap frog negotiations, 58

lend lease, 46, 57

Lenin, V. I. , 53, 113

liberalized trade and investment, 2

licensing, cooperation involving, 156

linkage diplomacy, 151; research in, 156

linkage, U. S. trade and foreign policy, 145

MacGregor, Clark, 15

Maisonrouge, Jacques G. , 7, 62

major historical developments, post-World War II, 64

Malek, Frederic V. , 81

Malenbaum, Wilfred, 111

manufacturers, definition, 4

Mao Tse-tung, 43

Marchetti, Victor, 73

Marine Cargo Insurance Industry, 58

market development cooperators, 98

market development program, 98

Marks, John D. , 73

Marshall Plan, 43

Marx, Karl, 113

mass appeals, 141

materials, demand for, 112

Meany, George, 2, 148

membership groups, 23

Modelski, George, 41

MNB: activist role, 110; agenda
    formulators, 1; and edu-
    cation, 34; and job exper-
    ience, 33; and job respon-
    sibility, 34; as global
    administrators, 24; as
    independent information
    base, 57; as information
    source, 147; as political
    actors, 58; as strategists
    and planners, 79; by age
    group, 33; contribution,
    evaluated by bureaucrats,
    131; defined, 10; impact of,
    147; influencing export
    licenses, 135; informal,
    direct ties with bureaucrats,
    138; input on U.S. grain
    policy, 98; instruments of
    influence, 1; interest group
    identification, 58; inter-
    national politician , 5; inter-
    viewed by company type, 32;
    lobbying activities, 2;
    positions held, 120; private
    foreign policy makers, 1;
    role in conduct of U.S.
    foreign policy, 116, 120, 142;
    role in politics, 84; state-
    less individuals, 9; types
    contacting government
    officials, 129; unintentionally

MNB (con't)
    stimulate social group
    representatives, 2

MNB's contacts with competitor
    MNCs, 126; contacts, nature
    of, 123; general character-
    istics, 24-25; motivations,
    21; personality affects U.S.
    foreign policy, 24; role
    possibilities, 25

MNC as instrument of neo-colonial-
    ism, 9; international pro-
    ducing, distributing institution,
    9-10

MNCs as quasisovereigns, 9;
    challenge nation-state's
    legitimacy, 14; cooperative
    agreements with the Soviet
    Union, 53; kinds defined, 28;
    sales figures, 28; type
    defined, 28

Mobil Oil, policy ads, 15

modern capitalism, 3

most-favored-nation status, 57

multilateral diplomatic problem
    solving, 16-17

multinational cluster, 3

multinational corporation, defined, 3

multinational enterprise, coordi-
    nator role, 63

Multinational Executives' Council on
    Foreign Relations, 149

multiregional corporations, 4

Murphy Commission Report, 64

National Airlines, 73

National Machine Tool Builders
    Association, 58

national self-interest, 11

nation-state weaknesses, 41

negotiating agreements, 153

Nixon, Richard M. , 43, 46, 81

nondemocratic political style, 11

normalization of economic
    relations, 44

Norstad, Lauris, 133

Nye, Joseph S., Jr., 14

Occidental Petroleum, 53, 114

oil meal exports, U.S. to
    Eastern Europe, 91

OPIC, 55

patents, protecting, 73

peer group pressure, 146

Pepsico, Inc. , 12

Perlmutter, Howard V. , 8

personal ties, 144

petroleum, 4

Pisar, Samuel, 113, 134

plant, production lines, supply
    of, 156

Poland, U.S. investment in, 54

political actors, U.S. MNBs
    as, 74

Policy Advisory Committee for
    Trade Negotiations, 70

policy differences, bureaucrats
    and MNBs, 127; methods used
    to resolve, 126, 127

political constraints, 4

political roles of MNBs, 146

position, concept of, 6

postindustrial society, 120

Powell, Reed, 23-24, 26

pretest interviews, 38

private sector advisory com-
    mittees, 70

probability sample, 6

professional generalist manager, 82

professional ties, 138

prospective joint venture invest-
    ment projects, 53

publicity, U.S.-Soviet grain
    purchases, 94

Public Law 480, 98

Public Law 93-618, 70

reference groups, 23-24, 146

reformulating policy, 126

regional corporations, 4

Remmers, H. Lee, 12

research and development, 157

research model, 27

research, recommendations for,
    151

research questions, 20

Richardson, John, Jr., 16

Robert Nathan Associates, 133

Robinson, Charles W. , 88

Rockefeller, David, 131, 141

role behavior, 22

role conflict, 12, 144, 147

role, defined, 12, 21

role, explanations of, 144-45

role of MNB, in U. S. commercial relations, 68

role relationships, 12

roles, bureaucrats feel MNBs
play in U. S. foreign policy,
143; MNBs feel they play in
U. S. foreign policy, 142

role types, 15, 142

Rolfe, Sidney, 9

Romania, U. S. joint venture
investments, 54-55

Rostow, Eugene V. , 133

rule-making procedures, 153

sales, 707s in Eastern Europe,
58

SALT agreements, 44, 151

sample criteria, 32

sampling generalizability, 6

Sampson, Anthony, 1

Schoonover, David M. , 94

Schultz, George, 129

Schumpter, Joseph A. , 13

selected articles on U. S. MNBs

and politics, 26

semiconductor industry, 104; market in Eastern Europe, 105

Shetty, Y. K. , 21

Shields, Roger F. , 102

Shulman, Marshall D. , 44

Sisco, Joseph J. , 16

Skolnikoff, Eugene B. , 42

social psychology concepts, 6

sovereignty, challenge to nation
state, 69

Soviet agriculture, 89

Soviet-U. S. grain sales, 151

Soviet commodity purchasing
program, 91

Soviet feedgap, 94

Soviet grain harvest, 89; imports,
89

Soviet hegemony, 40

Soviet Jewish emigration, 47-48

Soviet Union, 2; U. S. investment
in, 55-56

Soviet wheat purchases, 89

State Department conservatism,
rigidity, 76

State Department Office of Private
Cooperation, 15

status, concept of, 6

Stolte, Darwin, 99

strategic controls, 94

structured interview schedule, 38

style, policy making, 147

subcontracting, 155

Swindell-Dressler, 114

task forces, 70

TASS, 48

technology, advanced, 102

technology transfer, 14, 148

Tito, Marshall, 111

Trade Reform Act, 1973, H.R. 10710, 2, 57, 70

trade associations, examples of, 132-34, 135, 137

trade, element of detente, 147-48

trademarks, protecting, 73

traders, definition, 4

transnational organizations, 67, 148

transporters, definition, 4

Trezise, Phillip H., 133

Trowbridge, Alexander B., 133

UN Commission on Transnational Corporations, 2

UNESCO, 2

unintended direct role, 1

UN Resolution 1913, 2

UN Secretary general, 2

U.S. agricultural exports, 99

U.S. businessmen in Moscow, needs of, 57

U.S. Chamber of Commerce, 136, 145

U.S. diplomacy, nature of, 63

U.S. diplomats, attributes of, 75; members of a professional group, 75

U.S. direct investments abroad by major industry, 52

U.S. economic interdependence, 64

U.S. foreign policy explanations, 41

U.S. government agencies sampled, 31

U.S. government departments in East-West trade, 35

U.S. government officials, 121

U.S. government investment policy in Eastern Europe, groups used by MNBs to effect changes, 136

U.S. grain commodities, 94

U.S. investment, future in Eastern bloc, 110

U.S. MNBs, attributes of, 77; attributes of manager, 78; decision process, 80-81; failure in government service, 81; operating styles, 80-81; specialized functions, 79; tasks of, 78

U.S. raw material imports, 12

U.S.-Soviet agreements, implementation, 116

U.S.-Soviet fertilizer plants, 53

U.S.-Soviet trade, 47; figures, 48; major commodities, 50

U. S. technology, 47

U. S. / USSR agricultural coop-
      eration, 100-01

USSR feed trade, 94

USSR loans, 112

Venu, S. , 9

Weinberger, Caspar, 129

WJS Incorporated, 133

worldwide corporations, 3

Washington Energy Conference, 17

Yugoslavia, U. S. joint venture
      investment, 55

JEFFREY M. BROOKSTONE is a former research associate, Woodrow Wilson International Center for Scholars, The Smithsonian Institution, Washington, D. C. He received his Ph. D. in International Relations from The George Washington University. His fields of study were international business, economics, politics, communications, and U. S. foreign policy.

Dr. Brookstone previously worked on the staff of U. S. Senator Paul H. Douglas and the staff of the Joint Economic Committee. He is a member of the Academy of International Business and the International Studies Association. He resides in Washington, D. C. , and is a private consultant and lecturer.

EAST-WEST BUSINESS TRANSACTIONS
edited by Robert Starr

FOREIGN TRADE AND U. S. POLICY: The Case
for International Trade*
Leland B. Yeager and
David G. Tuerck

INTERNATIONAL REGULATION OF
MULTINATIONAL CORPORATIONS
Don Wallace, Jr.

THE MULTINATIONAL CORPORATION AS A FORCE
IN LATIN AMERICAN POLITICS: A Case Study of
the International Petroleum Company in Peru
Adalberto J. Pinelo

MULTINATIONAL CORPORATIONS AND
EAST EUROPEAN SOCIALIST ECONOMIES
Geza P. Lauter and
Paul M. Dickie

MULTINATIONAL CORPORATIONS AND GOVERNMENTS:
Business-Government Relations in an International Context
edited by Patrick M. Boarman
and Hans Schollhammer

THE NATION-STATE AND TRANSNATIONAL CORPORATIONS
IN CONFLICT: With Special Reference to Latin America
edited by Jon P. Gunnemann

NATIONAL CONTROL OF FOREIGN BUSINESS ENTRY:
A Survey of 15 Countries
Richard D. Robinson

THE POLITICAL ECONOMY OF EAST-WEST TRADE
Connie M. Friesen

*Also available in paperback as a PSS Student Edition